D0871172

The Stained Glass
HOME

GEORGE W. SHANNON & PAT TORLEN

Sterling Publishing Co., Inc. New York
A Sterling/Tamos Book

A Sterling/Tamos Book

Sterling Publishing Co., Inc.
387 Park Avenue South, New York, NY 10016-8810

Tamos Books Inc.
300 Wales Avenue, Winnipeg, MB Canada R2M 2S9

10 9 8 7 6 5 4 3 2 1

Design Alice Crawford & Stephanie Whitehouse
Photography Jerry Grajewski, grajewski·fotograph·inc.

Library and Archives of Canada Cataloging in Publication Data

Shannon, George (George Wylie), 1961-
   Stained glass home,the / George W. Shannon and Pat Torlen
 "A Sterling/Tamos book".
 Includes index.
 ISBN 1-895569-59-1
 1. Glass Craft –Patterns 2. Mosaics 3. Glass painting and
staining –Patterns   I. Torlen, Pat, 1960- II.Title.
TT298.S53 2005   748.5'028'5   C2005-906452-8

Tamos Books Inc. acknowledges the financial support of the
Government of Canada through the Book Publishing
Development Program (BPIDP) for our publishing activities.

ISBN-13: 978-1-85569-59-9
ISBN-10: 1-895569-59-1

For information about custom editions, special sales, premium
and corporate purchases, please contact Sterling Special Sales
Department at 800-805-5489 or specialsales@sterlingpub.com.

Dedication

For our staff and fellow artists who help make On The Edge Glass Studio an exciting and creative place to spend time.

Acknowledgments

Special thanks to
• Len Dushnicky, Michelle Gaber, Susan Green, Wendy Meyer, and Brianna Stark for their creative input and assistance in constructing the projects in this book.
• The moms — Betty Shannon and Hanna Torlen — for always being there and having a car to lend us at a moment's notice.

Notes

• All projects in this book are original, copyrighted designs by On The Edge Glass Studio.
• The projects in this book are not recommended for children under the age of 12 years. Children ages 12 to 16 should have adult supervision when working on projects described in this book.

Table of Contents

ABOUT THE AUTHORS 4
INTRODUCTION 5
MOSAIC CONSTRUCTION 6
MATERIALS 6
TOOLS 9
THE WORK AREA 12
SAFETY PRACTICES AND EQUIPMENT 13

BASIC TECHNIQUES 14
Choosing Mosaic Materials for a Project 14
Making Copies of Patterns 14
Transferring Pattern Shapes onto
   Glass 15
Cutting and Shaping Glass 16
Practice Patterns 21
Making Stained Glass Tesserae 22
Cutting & Shaping Tesserae, China,
   & Other Mosaic Materials 23
Smoothing Jagged and Sharp Edges
   on Mosaic Pieces 24

MOSAIC CONSTRUCTION TECHNIQUES 26
Direct Method – Basic Steps 26
Indirect (Reverse) Method – Basic Steps 32
Base/Support Structures 35
Care & Maintenance of Finished Mosaic Projects 37

MOSAIC PROJECTS AND PATTERNS 38
Baby's First ABCs wall plaques 39
Shining Stars wall clock & plaques 41
Man in the Moon wall hanging 45
Bonsai tea tray 47
Rocky Raccoon wall hanging 51
Dream wall hanging 53
Serenity birdbath 57
Prairie Vista Triptych wall hangings 61
Birch Grove cabinet door panel 63
Heartbeat wall mirror 67
Inukshuk Panorama wall hanging 70
A Safe Place curio cabinet 73

A Boy & His Dragon trio 75
   • shield mirror 76
   • sword clothes rack 78
   • dragon bookcase/cupboard 80
Rose Nouveau tabletop 83
Wright Style duo 86
   • headboard 87
   • nightstand 90
Phoenix Rising garden marker 93

TRANSLUCENT MOSAICS 95
   The Basic Steps 95

TRANSLUCENT MOSAIC
PROJECTS AND PATTERNS 97
   Things with Wings bugmobile 99
   Blue-Eyed Daisy decorative plate 103
   Butterfly Swoop window hanging 105
   Dragonfly divider 107

GLASS MOSAIC GARDEN STONES 110
The Basic Steps 110
Help! Why Didn't My Garden Stone Turn Out? 116
Making Custom Garden Stone Forms/Molds 118

GARDEN STONE PROJECTS AND
PATTERNS 120
Autumn Oak Leaf 121
Luna Moth 123
Herb Garden Collection 125
   • Basil 125
   • Chives 126
   • Lavender 126
   • Mint 126
   • Parsley 126
   • Sage 126 ·
   • Sweet Woodruff 126
   • Violet 126
Metric Conversion Chart 128
Index 128

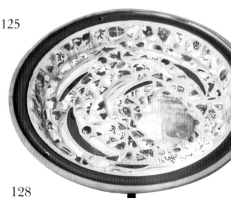

About the Authors

George W. Shannon's and Pat Torlen's fascination with glass began as a hobby and mutual interest. The hobby quickly evolved into a dual career change with the 1992 opening of their business, On The Edge Glass Studio, in Winnipeg, Canada. Pat and George design and fabricate commissioned works for commercial and residential clientele utilizing traditional and contemporary stained glass techniques, sandblasting, kiln work, and mosaic construction. In 1999, they were commissioned to create a sandcarved and airbrushed glass wall for Air Canada's Maple Leaf lounge at the Winnipeg International Airport. The Trinity Series of communion chalices and vessels they created for the Parish of St. Timothy received a 1999-2000 Modern Liturgy Visual Arts Award. In 2002/2003, On The Edge Glass Studio designed and produced two large commissioned works for clients in the United States. Stained glass doors and windows were created for the private dining room at Beaver Run Ski Resort in Breckinridge, Colorado. Several sandcarved door panels and a sandcarved and airbrushed glass wall, complete with passage door and kiln-formed waterfall, were created for the great room of an exclusive Florida home overlooking the Gulf of Mexico. They are now in the design and fabrication phases of a large fused glass donor wall and skylight installation for the new entrance to St. Boniface General Hospital in Winnipeg.

George and Pat find teaching to be rewarding and inspirational. Many new and wonderful designs and techniques come to fruition because of the challenges put forth by their students and the efforts made to provide instruction that is both informative and fun for students and instructors alike. Through the years, both artists have expanded their repertoire of skills by participating in intensive workshops and classes given by internationally renowned glass artists. George has attended Pilchuck Glass School in Stanwood, Washington while Pat attended Bullseye Glass Company's instructors course for glass fusing techniques. She was a coordinator and participant in the glass casting session taught by Irene Frolic at the University of Manitoba.

This is the sixth book authored by George and Pat and published by Sterling/Tamos. The previous five titles are: Stained Glass Projects & Patterns; Stained Glass Mosaics Projects & Patterns; Decorative Glass: Sandblasting, Copper Foil & Leaded Stained Glass Projects & Patterns (released in softcover as The New Stained Glass: Techniques, Projects, Patterns & Designs); Marvelous Mosaics With Unusual Materials; and The Stained Glass Garden Patterns & Projects. Pat and George are currently working on their seventh glass crafting project and pattern book. The upcoming book will feature a new collection of stained glass lamps and large panels for windows, doors, and room dividers. For more information about their studio, books already in print, and their upcoming new titles, visit www.ontheedgeglass.com.

Introduction

For several thousand years mosaic art, which is characterized as a surface decoration made by inlaying small pieces of colored glass or stone to form figures or patterns, has graced our homes, public spaces, and sacred structures. Style, substance, and popularity may have changed and evolved many times over but one factor remains constant – designs and images are brought to new life as light dances along the surfaces of the many pieces that comprise a mosaic. New dimensions are revealed as light is reflected, transmitted, and transformed upon striking the varied textures and colors of the tesserae, also known as the many individual units of a mosaic.

Traditionally, mosaics were fabricated by skilled craftsmen adhering small cubes of glass, marble, and ceramic or stone tiles, pebbles, and semi-precious stones to a relatively flat surface. Mosaic wall murals and floor installations were often complex and intricate in designs depicting myths, religious allegories, or interpretations of paintings by famous artists. While the popularity of mosaic art has waxed and waned over the centuries, it is currently in a period of high interest and transformation.

Artists, craftsmen, and hobbyists are exploring the unlimited possibilities for creative and functional expression that mosaic construction offers.

Ordinary household items such as china and glassware are now among the materials employed as tesserae and support structures. With tools and materials commonly found in the home workshop or at the local hardware store or home and garden center, getting started in basic mosaic construction is simple and fun.

Many stained glass enthusiasts have taken up this exciting craft adapting their tools and a wonderful selection of art glass to create mosaics.

Many of the featured projects in this how-to guide were created using stained glass materials and techniques but are easily adapted to suit available materials and to individual skill levels.

There are 23 projects plus 10 garden stone patterns in this book offering detailed instructions for crafting mosaics. The patterns can be adapted to suit any size or type of project and will hopefully serve as inspiration for future designs. Take a trip to your local library or bookstore to read up on the fascinating history of the art of mosaics and see photographs illustrating the accomplishments of great artists and craftsmen. There is a wealth of information available offering ideas and inspirations.

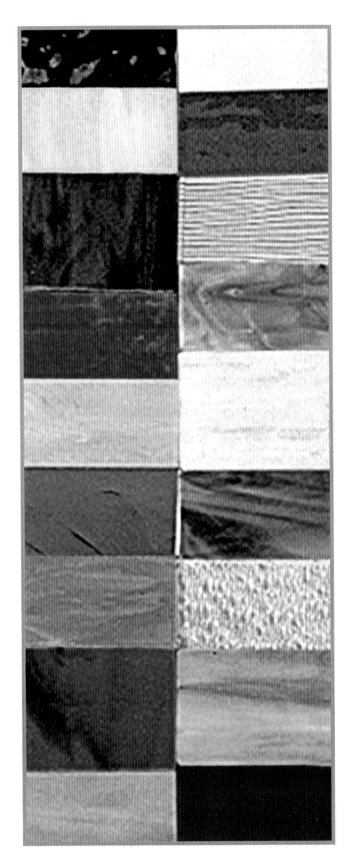

Mosaic Construction

Many of the materials and tools necessary for crafting mosaic art pieces are commonly found around the home and at local hardware stores or home and garden centers. Most urban centers have retail outlets that cater to hobbyists and stained glass artisans. These stores usually have knowledgeable staff that can give expert advice and recommendations for choosing proper tools and materials. Check telephone directory yellow pages for listings of local shops and establishments offering mail order service. Secondhand stores and garage sales are a great source for inexpensive materials that are unique and unusual. Artisans experienced in stained glass or mosaic fabrication are another informative resource when looking for supplies. A wide selection of tools and materials is available for every skill level. Finding the tool that best suits your needs and the right components to complete any project in this book should not be difficult.

Materials

Glass Many projects in this book have been constructed using art glass and mirrored glass instead of traditional tesserae materials. Once a few simple cutting techniques are mastered, glass is easy to cut and shape, and comes in an endless variety of color combinations.

Vitreous Glass Mosaic Tile These ³/₄ in square tesserae have a flat top surface, are uniform in size, and available in a wide selection of opaque colors and rich translucent shades with sparkling swirls of copper. The underside of each tessera has beveled edges and slight grooves to aid adhesion to the project base or support structure. These tiles are durable, will stand up to most climactic conditions, and are suitable for both indoor and outside mosaic projects.

Glass Nuggets, Marbles, and Jewels

These decorative glass pieces are used to accent and give detail to mosaic pieces and are found in a wide selection of colors, sizes, and shapes.

Ceramic Tile and Chinaware

There are infinite varieties of commercial ceramic mosaic tiles available. Tiles are sold individually or in manageable sheets held together with a paper or net backing. Sheets of tiles can be applied to cover large areas quickly or removed from the backing and used individually. Consider using specialty ceramic tiles or pieces of household china and crockery to accent mosaic projects.

Stone

Pieces of marble, slate, granite, and other stone materials as well as pebbles and small rocks can be used to add points of interest to a mosaic design.

Found Objects

Collect interesting bits of beach glass, shells, fossils, wire, jewelry pieces, and other mementos and souvenirs to personalize a special mosaic project.

Adhesive

There are many types of adhesive and glue for bonding the pieces of a mosaic to the base or support structure. Read labels carefully when choosing a suitable adhesive for the project you are working on. The base material (what you are bonding the glass to), the location, and purpose of the finished mosaic must all be taken into consideration. Use a non-toxic adhesive whenever possible.

• Mastic is premixed glue used to adhere tiles for interior wall applications. Many featured projects (such as wall hangings) will require this commonly used adhesive to adhere glass and other types of tesserae.

• Thin-set mortar is comprised of Portland cement, sand, and water. Liquid latex polymer additive can be used instead, or in combination with, water for greater strength, flexibility, and impact resistance. Thin-set mortar is essential for

floors, outdoor installations, and any application that requires a degree of water-resistance.

• Clear silicone is used for translucent mosaic projects. When applied correctly, clear silicone is a strong bonding agent that should not be visible between the transparent glass pieces and supporting glass sheet or structure.

• All purpose white glue and carpenter's glue are non-toxic and are suitable for small indoor projects including wall hangings, plaques, and trivets.

Grout Grout is used to fill the interstices (spaces) between individual mosaic pieces. In addition to giving the project a finished look, grout gives additional strength, covers sharp tesserae edges, and helps to level the mosaic surface. Grout comes in many colors or tints can be added to create the desired shade. Consider the site and use for your project when choosing a grout.

Pre-mixed Mortar Cement Found at hardware stores and home and garden centers, pre-mixed mortar cement is used to produce the mosaic garden stone projects. A mixture of Portland cement and sand, the addition of water and/or a liquid latex polymer additive is all that is needed to produce a fine grade of mortar cement to give the garden stone surface a smooth, even finish. For additional strength and durability, mix additional Portland cement (the bonding agent) into the cement mixture.

Tint Tint can be added to grout and cement to achieve a color that is not readily available. There are many types, in powder or liquid form, made specifically for these products. Colored latex and acrylic paints can also be used to tint cement.

Sealant Apply sealant to protect grout and mosaic surfaces from moisture damage and scuff marks. Porous materials such as unglazed ceramic tile, terra cotta, marble, slate, limestone, etc. should be sealed before grouting to avoid staining. Many interior projects including wall hangings and translucent mosaics will not require a sealant. Choose the sealant appropriate for each specific project. Re-application of sealant may be required periodically to compensate for climate and day-to-day wear.

Petroleum Jelly A thin layer of petroleum jelly is rubbed onto the sides and bottom of a mosaic garden stone form or mold before wet cement is poured into it. The jelly makes for easy removal of the garden stone from the mold.

Clear Adhesive-Backed Vinyl For the indirect method of mosaic construction, a sheet of clear adhesive-backed vinyl is used to hold the tesserae in place to prevent movement of the pieces while assembling a mosaic or when pouring the cement for a garden stone. After laying the mosaic pattern down on the work surface, the adhesive-backed vinyl (sandblasting resist, mosaic mount, or contact paper) is cut to the overall size and shape of the mosaic. The wax paper backing is removed and the vinyl is placed over the pattern with the adhesive back facing upward. The pattern can still be seen as the tesserae are laid onto the adhesive backing in the appropriate position.

Reinforcement Wire Mesh To add strength and durability to mosaic garden stones, a reinforcement wire mesh is added when the cement is poured. Use galvanized hardware cloth with $1/2$ in to 1 in mesh size.

Plywood and Wood Moldings To construct forms/molds/ or base support structures to complete projects, $1/2$ in to $3/4$ in exterior grade plywood and various wood moldings and trims may be required. Instructions and/or alternatives will be given where necessary.

Bases or Support Structures Mosaics can be created using many different types of bases or support structures to build upon. Ready-made wooden furniture, pre-cut mirrors, concrete pedestals and birdbaths, glass and china vessels, terra cotta pots, and picture frames are just a few of the items that can be used. Floor installations require cement backboard as the foundation for laying tiles and mosaics. Suggestions and ideas for bases are given with each project and instructions are supplied for constructing support structuress.

Tools

Permanent Waterproof Fine-tipped Marker This tool is used for outlining pattern pieces on glass to aid in cutting tesserae into specific shapes accurately. For dark and opaque glass, a silver, gold, or white marker works well.

China Marker Use a china marker to indicate where ceramic tiles and other porous mosaic materials need to be shaped and trimmed.

Drawing Equipment Small square, pencil, eraser, cork-backed ruler or straightedge, grid paper, tracing paper, carbon paper, marking pen, compass, scissors, light cardstock. Drawing materials and tools assist in making pattern copies, drawing and scoring straight lines, verifying angles and proper alignment, and making templates.

Traditional Glass Cutters A traditional glass cutter is required to accurately score and break individual pieces of glass to fit project patterns. The two most common types of glass cutters are dry wheel and oil-fed. An inexpensive steel wheel cutter has a larger steel cutting wheel and is usually disposed of after a few small projects. A lubricant must be applied to the steel wheel before each score is made. This type of cutter is a good choice for initial projects before making a decision about continuing with the craft. In comparison, self-lubricating cutters, which have smaller cutting wheels made of carbide steel and a reservoir for oil, are more expensive but last for many years. The smaller wheel can better follow the contours and uneven surfaces of art glass and is preferred by many artisans. Popular models have either a traditional pencil-shaped barrel or a pistol grip handle.

Glass Mosaic Cutters (also known as Nippers) This tool is designed to nip shapes from smaller pieces of glass. The plier-shaped

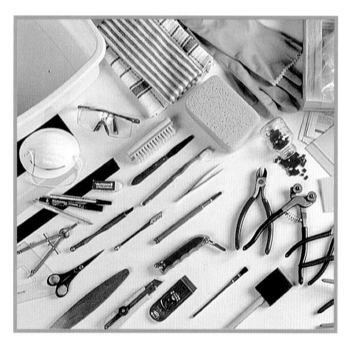

cutter has two long-lasting and replaceable carbide wheel jaws and is used scissor-like to cut and shape glass tesserae.

Breaking/Grozing Pliers Breaking pliers have flat smooth jaws that are well suited for gripping and breaking away scored pieces of glass and thin ceramic tiles. Grozing pliers have narrow, flat, serrated jaws to nibble away at unwanted bits along the edge of the glass so the piece will fit the pattern. Combination pliers combine the uses of breaking and grozing pliers. The top jaw is flat and the bottom jaw is concave – both are serrated. These are the most popular pliers for stained glass hobbyists.

Running Pliers Running pliers are ideal for scoring and breaking glass into multiple strips and smaller tesserae. These pliers are designed to apply equal pressure on both sides of the score line forcing the score to "run" or break along its length. They are used mainly for breaking score lines that are long and straight or gently curved. With practice, they can be used to start breaks on more difficult score lines. Metal running pliers have a concave jaw (placed on top

side of glass) and a convex jaw (placed on underside of glass) that allows the breaking of narrow pieces of glass. They also have the strength to carry a "run" over a longer distance. Some pliers have a central guide mark on the top jaw to assist in aligning the pliers on top of the glass correctly
(if absent, draw a guide mark with a permanent waterproof marking pen).

Tile Cutters There are a variety of tools for cutting tiles. Most are relatively inexpensive while larger items such as wet saws can be rented from a local home and garden center or equipment rental company.
- **Tile nippers** are similar to glass mosaic cutters and are effective for nipping out small curves and shapes.
- **A snap cutter** is used to score straight cuts and snap tile into two or more pieces.
- **Mini-cutters** resemble pliers but have a steel cutting wheel for scoring and jaws for snapping small tiles into smaller pieces.
- **A water-cooled wet saw** will cut tiles and stone quickly and accurately. Consider renting or purchasing a wet saw if the mosaic project is large scale and requires cutting many large pieces.

Carborundum Stone A small rectangular block composed of a hard carbon compound and silicon, the carborundum stone is used to file sharp edges off tesserae. The stone must be kept wet when smoothing the rough edges to keep minute particles from becoming airborne.

Diamond Pads These foam pads are impregnated with diamond particles and will remove sharp edges along the perimeter of tesserae. Always moisten the diamond pad with water when abrading glass or ceramic materials.

Wet/Dry Sandpaper This sandpaper is coated with silicon carbide. Moistened with water, it can be used to take the sharpness off rough tesserae edges.

Glass Grinder and Band Saw Complex and detailed glass shapes are now possible with the aid of a glass grinder or band saw. With its diamond-coated bit, a glass grinder can smooth rough and uneven edges and grind pieces of glass to fit a pattern accurately. Excess glass on tight inside curves can be ground away, reducing the risk of cracking a piece during the breaking or grozing process. A band saw with a diamond-coated blade will cut intricate glass shapes not otherwise achievable. Both machines have a reservoir containing water to trap the dust produced and prevent hazardous glass particles from becoming airborne.
NOTE *A glass grinder or band saw is not necessary to complete the glass mosaic projects though artisans with access to such equipment may wish to use it. A carborundum stone or wet/dry sandpaper may be used in most instances if some glass pieces require smoothing or a slight design change may be called for to simplify the cutting of a pattern piece.*

Small Containers or Jars Keep quantities of small tesserae organized. Sort the tesserae by color and size and store in small containers or jars.

Molds and Forms Many commercial molds and forms are available in the marketplace for the fabrication of mosaic garden stones. Some project patterns may be adapted to fit into such molds but instructions are included for making your own. Other easy and inexpensive alternatives include using plastic food storage containers and spring-form baking pans as garden stone forms. Secondhand shops and garage sales are great sources to hunt for inexpensive items that can be put to use as a form or mold.

Mixing Containers and Manual Mixers
Containers will be required when mixing cements and grouts. The container size will depend upon the quantities and volume of the materials to be mixed. An inexpensive manual cement mixer may be an item to invest in when making a number of mosaic garden stones. They save time and energy when mixing the quantities of cement required for larger garden stones.

Tweezers and Dental Tools These instruments are useful for the positioning of small pieces of tesserae on patterns and clear adhesive backed vinyl. Dental tools are useful for cleaning adhesives, cements, and grouts from small crevices and hard to reach corners.

Wire Cutters Also known as snips or side cutters, this tool will cut reinforcement wire mesh to the appropriate size and shape for the mosaic garden stones.

Trowel and Palette Knife These tools will enable you to apply and evenly spread adhesive. Apply adhesive to the base/support structure with the flat edge of a trowel, then make ridges with the notched side. Palette knives are used for buttering the back of tesserae, applying adhesive in hard-to-reach areas, and smoothing grout joints.

Sponges To prepare a project mosaic for grouting, wipe a water-moistened sponge across the surface of the mosaic. Upon completion of grouting, a damp sponge is necessary to wipe excess grout from mosaic surfaces before the grout is allowed to dry.

Brushes Small craft brushes are used to apply adhesive in small or hard-to-reach areas. In the final cleaning stages, a variety of brushes and old toothbrushes aid in the removal of excess dried grout and the surface polishing of the finished project.

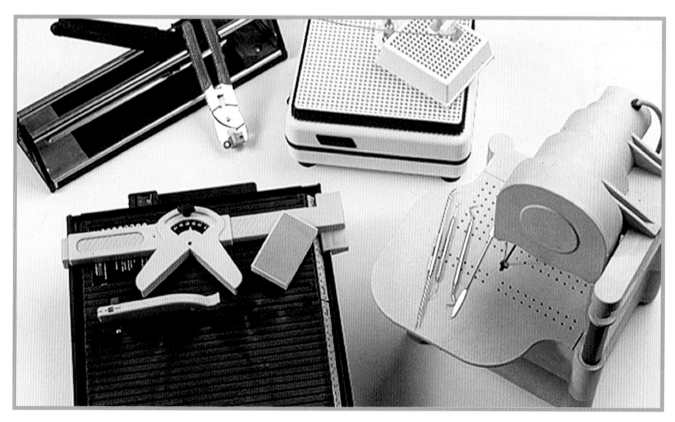

Utility Knife Use the utility knife for trimming the clear adhesive-backed vinyl, cutting out paper pattern templates, clearing away excessive adhesive and grout, etc.

Razor Blades/Paint Scrapers Use fresh blades to scrape away excess adhesive, grout, and cement from mosaic surfaces.

Polishing Cloths Clean and dry lint-free cloths are used to buff mosaic surfaces. Cloths made from cotton and other natural fibers are preferred.

Newspaper Protect work surface with newspaper. Rubbing the surface of a finished mosaic garden stone with newspaper lifts and removes debris while polishing at the same time. Newspaper is not recommended for the cleaning of light colored grouts.

Woodworking Tools Although many projects can be made with pre-fabricated molds or bases, a variety of woodworking tools is required to make your own. Where applicable, a list of required tools, materials, and instructions is supplied for the construction of forms and bases for specific projects.

The Work Area

Choose a comfortable working space with enough room to spread out the project. A proper and safe working area requires these items:
• large, sturdy table or workbench with a smooth, level work surface (preferably plywood) at comfortable working height (around waist level).
• abundant overhead lighting (natural light if possible).
• at least one electrical outlet with a grounded circuit for a glass grinder and/or wet saw.
• easy-to-clean hard surface floor.
• racks or wooden bins with dividers to store sheets of glass in an upright position. This helps to prevent scratching of glass surfaces. Store smaller pieces in a cardboard box.
• proper ventilation (window, fan) when working with adhesives, grouts, and cements.
• supply of newspaper to cover work surface and for easy cleaning.
• bench brush and dust pan to clear work surface of glass chips and other debris.

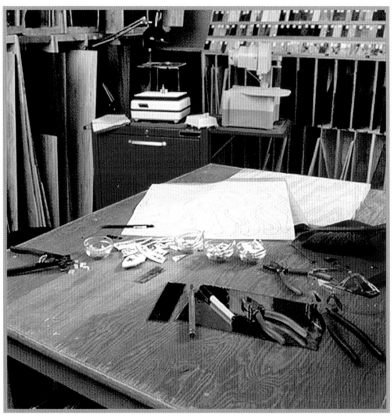

• access to water for mixing grouts and cements, using grinding or cutting equipment, and cleaning projects.

NOTE *It is recommended that mixing concrete be done outdoors whenever possible. This will prevent the active ingredients and dust in the cement mixture from entering the work area and/or home.*

Safety Practices and Equipment

To work safely while constructing mosaic projects, there are several items that should always be present and used when appropriate: safety glasses or goggles, work apron, rubber or latex gloves, respirator or dusk mask, hearing protection.

Follow these simple rules to ensure a safe and healthy work environment.

• Always wear safety glasses or goggles when cutting glass and tesserae to prevent the risk of eye injury due to small fragments that may become airborne during cutting.

• Protect your clothing by wearing a full-length work apron at every stage of the mosaic construction process.

• Wear closed shoes to prevent glass fragments and cement powders from coming in contact with your feet.

• Pre-mixed mortar cement compounds form a caustic, calcium hydroxide solution when mixed with water. When handling cement powders and the wet mixtures, avoid contact with skin or eyes by wearing tight-fitting safety glasses or goggles, rubber or latex gloves, and protective clothing (long sleeve work shirts and full length pants are recommended).

• Use soap and water to thoroughly wash any skin area and clothing that comes in contact with wet cement mixtures or concrete. Wash work clothes and aprons separately from other clothing.

• Wear a dust mask or respirator when handling or mixing cement and grout powders. Visit your local safety supply store for pertinent information on respirators and filters.

• Work outdoors or in a well-ventilated area when mixing cement or working with adhesives. Whenever possible, use materials that are non-toxic.

• To avoid the possibility of ingesting cement and grout dusts and powders, do not eat, drink, or smoke while working with these materials. Keep hands away from mouth and face and wash exposed skin areas with soap and water.

• Cover all cuts and scrapes with an adhesive plaster when working with cement or grout to prevent skin irritation.

• Clean work area and floor surface with a damp mop or wet sponge to prevent cement and grout powders and dusts from becoming airborne.

• Carry large glass pieces in a vertical position with one hand supporting the sheet from below and the other hand steadying the sheet from the side. Wear protective gloves when moving larger sheets.

• Wear hearing protection when using loud machinery such as a wet saw.

Basic Techniques

Choosing Mosaic Materials for a Project

The selection of materials is an interesting and challenging aspect of any project. The varying combinations of design, color, texture, and light determines the look of a finished mosaic piece. Here are a few helpful guidelines.

• View mosaic materials in lighting conditions similar to those where the finished project will be displayed. Most materials should be chosen for the reflective quality of the top surface. For translucent glass mosaics, sheets of art glass are selected based on the ability to transmit light and color.

• Choose opaque materials that will obscure the adhesives and cements used to glue tesserae to the base and/or support structure of the mosaic. When making translucent mosaics, select cements, adhesives, or grouts that will not affect the color of the glass pieces and are the least visible. Consider using art glass with a textured and/or iridescent finish to camouflage the adhesive beneath it.

• Vibrant and colorful materials make a mosaic piece come alive. The larger the dimensions of a project, the greater the number of color variations, textures, and materials that can be introduced. Focus on 2 or 3 selections for small projects. If a wider range is desired, try varying shades or textures of the dominant tesserae. View the materials side by side to see how the colors and textures affect each other. Take into consideration the color of grout or cement used for the project.

• For the garden stone projects, it is recommended that at least one side of the mosaic material surface be as smooth and flat as possible. Heavily textured tesserae may not stick as readily to the adhesive-backed vinyl and may become partially or completely engulfed in the cement.

NOTE *Material quantities listed for individual projects are a close approximation for each pattern. Have additional material on hand to allow for matching patterns, grains and textures, or for possible breakage.*

Making Copies of Patterns

Prepare 2 or 3 pattern copies for the project you are working on. Compare each copy to the original pattern to ensure accuracy.

Photocopying
This is the easiest method to duplicate copies. Digital photocopiers make copies true to the original pattern and most copiers have the ability to enlarge or reduce patterns.

Tracing
Lay tracing vellum over the pattern and trace the lines of the design. Make more than 1 copy at a time by using carbon sheets. Lay a sheet of paper on the work surface and place a carbon face down overtop. For each additional copy required, add another layer of paper and carbon. Place the project pattern on top and fasten in place with

pushpins or tape. Trace the outline of the pattern, pressing firmly so that the image is transferred through to each layer of paper.

Blueprinting

Trace the pattern onto drawing vellum and take it to a blueprinting firm to make exact copies. If a pattern requiring mosaic pieces of a specific size and/or shape is reduced or enlarged, verify that these pieces fit the pattern before starting the project. Alter the pattern if necessary.

Overhead and Opaque Projectors

Projectors can be used to enlarge pattern designs, but patterns may be distorted and require adjustments. Use this method as a guideline only. When enlarging patterns with pieces that must be a certain size and/or shape, the pattern will have to be altered accordingly.

Grid Method

Grid work can be used to enlarge, reduce, or change the dimensions of a design. On paper large enough to accommodate the desired size, draw a new grid work with the size of the squares adjusted to fit the new grid. Copy the design from the original grid onto the modified one, square by square.

NOTE *For sizing reference, patterns in this book that are not full size are placed on grid work (1 square = 1 inch).*

HELPFUL HINTS
• Keep smaller patterns dry during the grinding stage by placing them inside vinyl sheet protectors or covering them with a clear adhesive-backed vinyl.
• When making multiple projects from one pattern, protect pattern copies by having them laminated.

Transferring Pattern Shapes onto Glass

Draw outline of the shape to be cut directly onto glass with a permanent waterproof fine-tipped

marker. Position pattern piece on glass sheet to avoid excessive waste but take into account the grain or texture of glass piece you are cutting and how it will flow with other mosaic pieces around it. Leave approximately $\frac{1}{4}$ in space around the piece so the breaking pliers will have material to grasp when breaking the score line.
• For many translucent and light-colored opalescent glasses, the pattern can be transferred by placing sheet of glass directly on the pattern copy and tracing the design lines with marker. A light box can help illuminate the pattern from

below when tracing onto darker shades of glass.
• For opaque glass, the pattern can be transferred onto the glass using one of three methods.

1 Using scissors or utility knife cut the required pattern piece from an extra copy of the project pattern. Place the pattern piece on the glass and trace around the outside edges with the marker.

2 Make a template of the pieces to be cut (using the tracing method described on p14) and use the marker to trace around the template perimeter onto the glass. Use cardstock, lightweight cardboard, or 2mm or 3mm float glass (clear window glass) for making the template. Use this method when making multiple projects using the same pattern.

3 Place a carbon sheet face down on the glass with the pattern on top. Press firmly with a pen or pencil to transfer the pattern lines onto the glass. Go over the carbon lines with marker.

NOTE *When cutting out a piece from the pattern copy or making a template, be sure to cut inside the pattern lines so the glass piece does not become larger than the pattern once it has been traced and cut.*

HELPFUL HINTS
• Dressmaker's carbon tracing paper comes in several colors other than the standard black and blue. Use a light color like yellow for tracing pattern shapes onto dark hued glass to make pattern lines more visible and easier to follow when cutting.
• Permanent markers may be difficult to see on dark shades of glass. Try using a silver, gold, or white paint marker for better visibility.

Cutting and Shaping Glass

Cutting Glass with a Glass Cutter
Cutting a piece of glass is the result of two separate actions – scoring and breaking. Once the requisite shape has been traced onto the glass with a permanent waterproof fine-tipped marker, the outline is scored by running the

The Basic Rules of Glass Cutting

• Wear safety glasses and a work apron. Stand in an upright position in front of the worktable.
• Work on a clean, level, non-skid work surface covered with newspaper.
• Always place the glass smooth side up, on which the pattern has been traced with the marker. Make sure the surface of the glass is clean and free of any debris.
• Hold the cutter in your writing hand perpendicular to the glass, not tilted to the left or right. Run the cutter away from your body and inside the pattern lines, applying steady pressure as you score the surface. The pressure should come mainly from your shoulder, not the hand. Lubricate the wheel of the cutter before each score if it is not a self-oiling model. How you hold the cutter in your hand will depend on what type is used and what grip is the most comfortable.
• Start and finish the score line at an edge of the glass. Do not stop or lift your cutter from the glass surface before the score is completed. Use a fluid motion, exerting constant, even pressure. Because of their shape, some pieces will require a series of scores and breaks.
• Never go over a score line a second time. To do so will compromise the score line and may damage the cutter wheel, increasing the likelihood of an unsuccessful break.
• To complete the break, grasp the glass with a hand on each side of the score line, thumbs parallel to the score, knuckles touching. Roll wrists up and outward, breaking the glass along the scored line.

wheel of a glass cutter along the traced line. Apply even pressure on either side of the score line to break the piece from the main sheet of the glass. Cutting glass properly is a skill that can be attained with a little effort and some practice. Draw cutting patterns A, B, C, and D (p21) on a 12 in by 12 in sheet of 3 mm float glass (clear window glass) and practice scoring and breaking before starting your first project. Use this exercise to practice cutting flow and amount of pressure to exert.

Breaking Glass Along a Score Line

Score lines are broken by hand as described above or with different types of pliers designed for the stained glass craft.

• Using Running Pliers

You will need these for making square and rectangular pieces required for some projects in this book. Running pliers are used for breaking straight lines. They can start a break at either end of slightly curved score lines. Metal running pliers are preferable. The slightly concave jaw must be placed on the topside of glass and convex jaw on the underside.

1 Position running pliers so score line is centered and glass is partially inside jaws, approx. $1/2$ in to $3/4$ in.

2 Gently squeeze handles and score will run (travel), causing the glass to break off into 2 pieces. If the run does not go the full length of score line, repeat procedure at other end of score line. The two runs should meet, causing the score line to break completely.

A Disposable cutters and oil-fed cutters are held in the traditional manner. The cutter rests between the index and middle fingers with the ball of the thumb placed to push the cutter along. The disposable cutter wheel must be lubricated before each score and wears out quickly.

B Pistol grip cutter held in palm of hand with the thumb resting on top of the barrel and index finger guiding cutter head.

C Pencil style cutter, oil-fed and held as a pencil.

D Break glass along the score line, as shown.

E & F For breaking straight lines or slight curves on glass, use the running pliers.

G & H Combination pliers or breaking pliers are positioned perpendicular to the score line.

I As a last resort, difficult to break glass may be tapped underneath the score line to urge the run to begin.

> Always start a score on one edge of the glass and complete the score at another edge.

- **Using Breaking Pliers or Combination Pliers**
Breaking pliers have 2 identical flat, smooth jaws that can be placed on either side of the glass. Combination pliers have a flat top jaw and a curved bottom jaw – both jaws are serrated.
1 Position pliers perpendicular to the score line and as close as possible without touching it. Start at either end of the score line (not the middle).
2 Use an out-and-downward pulling motion on the pliers to break the glass.
3 When using two sets of pliers to break apart two smaller pieces of glass, place pliers on the glass on either side of the score line and opposite to each other. Hold one set of pliers steady and use an out-and-downward pulling motion with the other set to separate the glass piece.

Breaking a Score Line by Tapping Underneath

Occasionally a score line will not break using your hands or a set of pliers. This may happen on long and/or curving score lines. Tapping may cause small chips and fractures along the score line and, if not done carefully, may result in the score running in a different direction than the one intended. The larger the glass piece being cut and the longer the score line, the greater the risk of an unsuccessful break. Use this method as a last resort.
1 Hold glass close to worktable surface. Using the ball end of the cutter, gently strike the glass from the underside, directly beneath the score line. Once the score begins to run, continue tapping ahead of the run until it reaches the other end of the score line.
2 Use your hands or a pair of pliers to separate the scored piece from the main sheet of glass.

Scoring a Straight Line

To score straight lines, the most consistent method is to use a cork-backed metal ruler with thick, rounded edges as a straightedge.
1 Mark the line to be cut and position straightedge parallel and approximately $^1/_8$ in from the line (exact distance is determined by the width of the cutter head).
2 Align the head of the glass cutter with the straightedge and position the wheel on one end of the marked line.
3 Holding the straightedge firmly against the glass surface, make the score line by either pulling the cutter toward the body or by pushing it away. Maintain even pressure throughout.
4 Break the score line, using the method you feel most comfortable with (p17,18).

Cutting Squares and Rectangles

It is almost impossible to score and break glass (by hand) at a 90° angle in one effort. Use a series of straight scores and breaks to cut square and rectangular pieces.
1 Trace pattern A (p21) onto glass, aligning one of the sides of the pattern with the edge of glass.
2 Score along the other side of the pattern piece and proceed to break the score line, using the method you prefer.
3 Score and break any remaining cut required to achieve the shape of the pattern piece.

Cutting Inside Curves

Inside curves are the most difficult cuts to score and break out successfully. Attempt the most

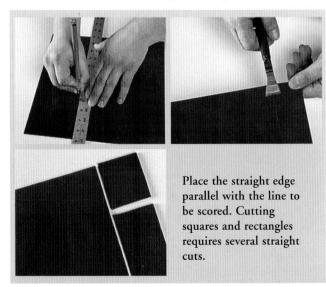

Place the straight edge parallel with the line to be scored. Cutting squares and rectangles requires several straight cuts.

difficult cut of a piece first, before cutting the piece away from the main sheet of glass.

1 Trace pattern piece B (p21) onto the glass. Position the outer edges of the curve so they align with the edge of the glass.

2 Score the inside curve of the pattern piece but do not attempt to break it out at this time.

3 Make several smaller concave score lines (scallops) between the initial score line and the outside edge of the glass.

4 Using breaker or combination pliers, start removing the scallops, one at a time, beginning with the one closest to the edge of the glass. Use a pulling action with the pliers rather than a downward motion. Remember to position the jaws of the pliers at either end of the score line and not in the middle.

5 Continue to break away the scallops until the initial score line is reached. Remove it and proceed to score and break away the pattern piece from the larger glass sheet.

NOTE *The tapping method (p18) can be used, with caution, to run a score line to break out pieces along larger inside curves.*

Cutting Circles, Ovals, and Outside Curves

1 Trace pattern C (p21) onto the glass, leaving $1/2$ in space from the outside edge of the glass.

2 Make an initial score line to separate the pattern piece from the sheet of glass. The score line will go from the outside edge of the glass to the circle and then follow its perimeter for a short distance before heading on a tangent to an opposing edge of the glass (see line 1). Break away this piece.

3 The second score line will follow around the circle for a short distance (approximately $1/6$ th of the perimeter) and then leave on a tangent to the outside edge (see line 2).

4 Repeat step 3, scoring and breaking the glass in a pinwheel fashion, until the circle shape has been formed (see lines 3, 4, 5, and 6).

5 Small jagged edges where a score line was started or ended can be ground off with a glass grinder (pp10,25), nibbled away with combination pliers (see Grozing, pp9,25) or filed off with a carborundum stone (pp10,25).

6 This method for cutting circular pieces can be adapted to cut outside curves and ovals.

Scoring and Breaking S-Shaped Curves

1 Trace pattern D (p21) onto the glass, placing one side against the edge of the glass.

Cutting inside curves requires a series of concave cuts. Attempt the most difficult cut before breaking the piece away from the main sheet of glass.

A series of breaks following the arrows on pattern C on page 21 will create circular and oval shapes.

2 Score the S-shape cut first.

3 Align the running pliers with the score line. Squeeze only hard enough to start the run. Repeat the procedure at the opposite end of the score line. If both runs meet, use your hands to separate the resulting 2 pieces. If the runs do not meet, gently tap along the score line (on the underside of the glass).

4 Score and break out remaining cuts.

Using Glass Mosaic Cutters

Glass mosaic cutters, also referred to as nippers, are used to cut and shape the smaller pieces required to make a mosaic project.

1 Use a glass cutter and breaking or running pliers to cut a strip or smaller piece of glass away from a larger sheet. The cut-away piece must be slightly larger than the pattern piece that you require.

2 With a permanent waterproof fine-tipped marker, trace outline of the piece onto glass.

3 Grip mosaic cutters in your writing hand and hold the glass in the opposite hand. Using a scissor-like motion, nip away portions of glass along the trace line until you have achieved the desired shape.

Using a Diamond Band Saw

Specially designed to cut glass, ceramic tile, and similar hard materials, the band saw has added new dimensions to stained glass and mosaic crafting. Its diamond-coated stainless steel blade is capable of cutting intricate pattern shapes not normally achievable with a glass cutter or tile and/or glass nippers. The sawing action of the cutting blade eliminates the need for smoothing edges of the piece. Several models are available and can be purchased at stained glass retail centers and through mail order or Internet services. Read manufacturer's instructions carefully before starting and follow all safety precautions. The band saw has a water reservoir to cool the blade and prevent glass dust from becoming airborne. Plug saw into a grounded

S-shaped curves may require starting runs at each end of the score line so the runs meet near the center.

Nippers are one of the most popular tools for making tesserae. The shapes are not always even which is in character with the art of mosaics.

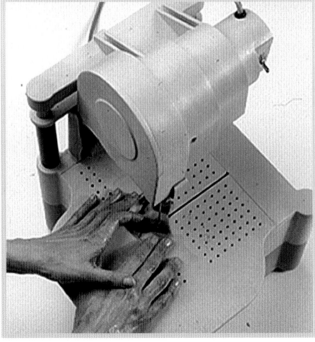

Practice Patterns

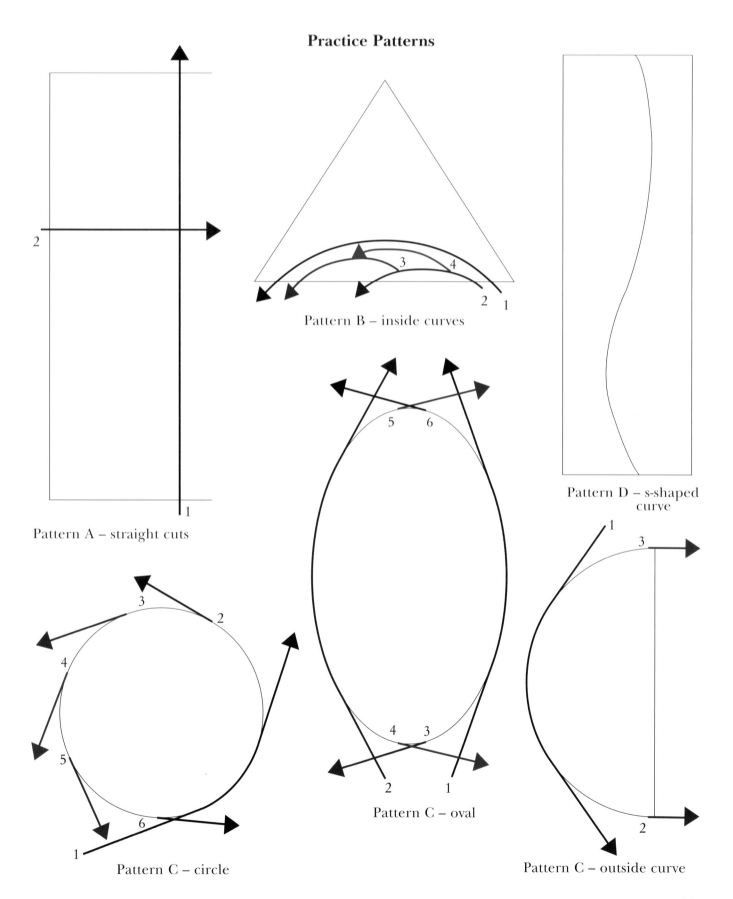

Pattern A – straight cuts

Pattern B – inside curves

Pattern C – oval

Pattern C – circle

Pattern D – s-shaped curve

Pattern C – outside curve

electrical outlet to avoid shocks.

1 Trace the pattern shape onto the glass or tile with a metallic paint marker or a thin-line paint marker. Allow the marker to dry before cutting to prevent water from washing away the outline. Alternatively, make a copy of the pattern piece from a clear overhead transparency sheet and secure it to the glass or tile surface with double-sided tape.

2 Place water in the reservoir and have a moistened sponge positioned adjacent to the diamond-coated blade at all times.

3 Cut along the pattern line (following the instructions provided by the manufacturer) until the desired shape has been attained. Allow space between each mosaic piece for the application of cement and/or grout.

4 Rinse each piece under clear running water to remove grit.

SAFETY NOTE *Always wear safety glasses when using any glass cutting or breaking tool.*

Making Stained Glass Tesserae

Many projects in this book require quantities of square or rectangular pieces to fill in areas and create borders. In traditional mosaic works, a small piece of colored glass used in this manner is referred to as a tessera (pl. tesserae). Use one of the two methods described below to make stained glass tesserae.

Cutting Uniform Tesserae

Cutting a sheet of glass into uniform 1 in by 1 in square tesserae is show this technique (see photos opposite). Adjust measurements to suit requirements for each project.

1 Cut a piece of glass 12 in by 12 in, making edges square.

2 Align a ruler along one side of the sheet of glass and make a mark on the edge of the glass at every 1 in interval.

3 Repeat step 2 on each of the four sides of the

Use a straightedge to accurately measure and mark the size of tesserae required onto the glass sheet. Score the marked sheet with a glass cutter and the straightedge. Use running pliers to break the scored lines into strips. Break strips into individual tesserae.

Use glass mosaic cutters to cut random glass strips into random-size tesserae.

glass sheet.

4 Align a cork-backed straightedge along the marks on two opposing sides and score a straight line (p18) at each 1 in interval with a glass cutter.

5 Repeat step 4 to make perpendicular score lines between the remaining two opposing sides. There should be a grid work of score lines visible on the surface of the glass.

6 With a pair of running pliers, break the score lines along one side, creating 12 – 1 in wide strips.

7 Take each strip and break the remaining score lines. There will now be 144 pieces of 1 in square tesserae.

> **HELPFUL HINTS**
> To make tesserae of varying amounts and sizes, simply adjust the size of the glass sheet and the intervals at which the sheet is to be scored.

Cutting Random-Size Tesserae

1 Use a glass cutter to randomly score lines from one edge of a small sheet of glass to the opposing side. Vary the angle and width between each score line while keeping the score lines no wider than 1 inch apart. The score line can be straight or slightly wavy.

2 Repeat step 1 to make perpendicular score lines between the remaining two opposing sides.

3 With a pair of running pliers, break the score lines along one side, creating long narrow strips.

4 Take each strip and break the remaining score lines into individual, random-size pieces.

> **HELPFUL HINTS**
> An alternative method is to cut narrow strips of glass and then proceed to nip the strips into smaller varying pieces with glass mosaic cutters.

Cutting and Shaping Tesserae, China, and Other Mosaic Materials

There are a variety of tools and techniques that can be employed to produce the individual pieces of a mosaic. While glass can be cut and shaped in a controlled manner and usually results in the size and shape required, other materials can be more unpredictable. Practice cutting and shaping techniques to become acquainted with tools and materials before starting a project. Always wear safety glasses and a work apron when cutting or shaping mosaic

Tesserae can be cut and shaped with tile nippers, glass cutter, snap cutter, or wet saw. When using tile nippers, the mosaic material should not be inside the jaws more than $1/8$ in.

Use nippers to trim a piece to form a specific shape.

Break ceramic into smaller segments with a hammer.

material. Use a china marker on porous materials to indicate areas that require trimming. Permanent marking pens may stain these surfaces.

Hammer
If size and shape are not a priority, a swift hit with a carpenter's hammer will quickly reduce a piece of china or ceramic tile into smaller segments. Place the object into a sturdy bag or an old pillowcase to contain shards and flying debris.

Tile Nippers
Tile nippers are used to cut and shape tile and ceramic materials into the smaller pieces. Tile nippers are a plier-like tool with tungsten carbide jaws and are indispensable for cutting clay-based materials.

- **Cutting mosaic tiles into smaller sections**

1 Grip the tile nippers in your writing hand and hold the tile, glazed side up, in the opposite hand.

2 Position the tile between the jaws of the nippers overlapping the tile edge approximately $1/8$ in. The jaws should be perpendicular to the tile edge.

3 Using a scissor-like motion, squeeze handles together in a single motion to snap tile into 2 pieces.

- **Cutting a specific size and shape**

1 Use a china marker to mark the intended shape of the tile.

2 Using the technique described above, nibble away small portions of the tile until the desired shape is achieved.

Glass Cutter

A glass cutter can be used to score some tile and ceramic materials, especially to facilitate the cutting of slight curves or to separate large pieces into smaller segments before contouring into a specific shape. Refer to the glass cutting section (pp16–21) for detailed instructions about using a glass cutter.

1 Score the tile along the cut to be made on the glazed top surface of the piece.

2 Score a grid of lines on the section of the material to be removed. Use tile nippers or grozing pliers (p9) to carefully remove small bits, one piece at a time, until all unwanted material has been removed along the initial score line. The jaws of the tile nippers should overlap the edge of the piece by approximately 1/8 in and should run parallel to the score lines.

Snap Cutter

Use a snap cutter to make a series of straight cuts on a single tile or to cut quantities of tile in a short period of time.

1 Using a china marker, mark the tile to indicate where a cut is required.

2 Position the tile on the metal frame of the cutter and align the carbide-tipped cutter wheel or blade along the marked line. Use a light but steady pressure to score the tile by drawing the cutter wheel along the top of the tile in one even stroke.

3 Press down on the cutter handle to break the tile into two pieces along the scored line.

Mini-cutter

Designed to cut smaller tiles, a mini-cutter has a carbide steel cutting wheel at its head and plier-like handles to snap the tile in two.

1 With the glazed or smoothest side of the tile facing upward, score the tile with a single fluid motion.

2 Placing the scored tile in the jaws of the cutter, position the tile with the score line facing up and centered on the lower jaw.

3 Squeeze the handles together to break the tile along the score line.

Wet Saw

This stationary circular saw is equipped with a water-cooled abrasive blade and can cut large quantities of tiles that only require straight cuts. Most home and garden centers, hardware stores, or flooring centers rent out wet saws or will cut the tiles for a nominal fee. Read the instructions carefully and follow all safety precautions outlined by the manufacturer.

Smoothing Jagged and Sharp Edges on Mosaic Pieces

The pieces of a mosaic usually do not need to fit the pattern as precisely as is necessary to construct a stained glass window. Many stained glass hobbyists and artisans use glass grinders to smooth away jagged edges or shape glass pieces to accurately fit the pattern. For most mosaic works, a carborundum stone, wet/dry sandpaper, or a diamond pad can be used instead of a glass grinder to dull any sharp edges. If you can not contour a mosaic piece into the shape required, simply alter the pattern to accommodate the shape that you can achieve.

Grozing

The jagged edge of the glass along the score line can be chipped away, to some degree, by a process called grozing. Grasp the piece of glass firmly in one hand, place the combination pliers perpendicular to the edge of the glass, and drag the serrated jaws along the jagged edge in an up-and-down motion. Repeat until the edge is smooth.

Using a Carborundum Stone, Diamond Pad, or Wet/Dry Sandpaper

Carborundum stones and wet/dry sandpaper are stocked at most hardware stores. A carborundum stone is a thin rectangular block composed of a hard carbon compound and silicon. Wet/dry sandpaper is dark gray in color, comes in many grit sizes, and is much smoother to the touch than regular sandpaper. A sheet of wet/dry sandpaper can be cut into smaller pieces and/or attached to a sanding block for easy handling. Diamond pads are harder to obtain but can be found at lapidary shops, tile and flooring centers, or glass stores.

1 Wet the smoothing device and the mosaic piece with water. They must be wet at all times to help keep minute glass and clay particles and dust from becoming airborne.

2 Rub the device in a file-like motion along the edge of the mosaic piece that requires smoothing.

3 Rinse the piece and the device under running water to wash away gritty residue.

Using a Glass Grinder

1 Attach a face shield to the grinder and position a back splash along the back and sides of the grinder to contain any airborne glass chips and water overspray.

A Jagged edges of glass can be smoothed by grozing.
B Keep carborundum stone or diamond pad wet at all times when smoothing sharp edges. Rinse away glass residue when finished.
C File away the jagged edge holding the tool at a slight angle.

D & E Use a glass grinder to swipe along the edges of the glass to take away any sharp edges. Check each piece against the pattern and mark areas needing further grinding.

2 Keep water in the reservoir and have a moistened sponge positioned adjacent to the diamond-coated bit at all times.

3 Cut each glass piece on the inside of the pattern line to fit the pattern with a minimum of grinding and allow for cement or grout to fit between each piece. If the glass pieces fit the pattern but have sharp edges, make one quick swipe against the grinding bit on each edge of the glass to dull any sharpness. Only light pressure is required when pushing the glass against the bit.

4 If traces of the marked line are still visible on the piece, grind the edge to ensure an accurate fit within the pattern lines.

5 Check each piece against the pattern. If any part of the piece overlaps the pattern lines and there is not adequate spacing between pattern pieces, mark area with a permanent waterproof marker and grind away the excess.

6 Rinse each piece under clear running water when grinding is complete.

7 To ensure proper performance of the glass grinder, clean thoroughly and rinse the water reservoir after each use.

HELPFUL HINTS

To remove small chips that can occur along a ground edge, use a mirror-grinding bit. This diamond-coated bit has a groove that grinds edges of the glass at several angles, providing a smoother finish.

Mosaic Construction Techniques

Two traditional techniques, direct method and indirect (or reverse) methods, have been used around the world for centuries to create a diverse spectrum of mosaic art pieces and installations. Equipment innovations and an ever-expanding palette of materials allow today's artisans more opportunities to explore and create.

Direct Method

Tesserae are positioned and bonded directly to a base or support structure. Grout is then spread over the mosaic surface to fill the interstices (spaces) between individual tessera. This method utilizes mosaic materials that may vary in size and thickness and is often used to compose free-forming mosaic designs for wall murals and three-dimensional objects. The artist is able to view the project as it develops and make subtle changes in the placement or type of tesserae before the adhesive sets and the pieces are permanently adhered to the base or support structure. Reflective light accentuates the slightly uneven surface, making the design more dynamic and giving the mosaic more visual depth.

Indirect (or Reverse) Method

This technique produces a smooth and level mosaic surface. Tesserae are arranged and adhered face down onto a clear adhesive-backed vinyl sheet positioned over a reversed copy of the project pattern. A thin layer of adhesive is applied to base or support structure and vinyl sheet with attached tesserae is turned over and pressed to the adhesive. Once adhesive sets, the vinyl is peeled away and mosaic is grouted. A variation of indirect method is used to produce the mosaic garden stone projects (p110). A tesserae-laden vinyl sheet is placed at the bottom of a form or mold and covered with cement. The mosaic is revealed once cement hardens and the garden stone is released from the form/mold.

Direct Method — The Basic Steps

Listed on p27 are the basic materials and tools that are required to construct mosaic projects implementing the direct method. Additional listings with specific requirements are provided for each project.

Preparing the Pattern

1 Make 2 copies (pp14–15) of project pattern.
2 Verify that outline of pattern fits within the area on base or support structure to be covered with tesserae. Compare pattern copies to original to ensure accuracy. Adjust pattern and/or copies if alterations are required.
3 Use one pattern copy as a guide for cutting, breaking, and shaping mosaic pieces to the correct size and shape (pp16–26). Use second copy to cut out any pattern piece that requires a template p16 (e.g. for cutting opaque materials) remembering to cut inside pattern lines.

MATERIALS

- 2 copies of pattern
- Base or support structure for mosaic
- Sealant (optional)
- Carbon paper
- Masking tape
- Newspaper
- Mosaic materials for project –
  art glass, china, tiles, glass nuggets,
  marbles and jewels, found objects, etc.
- Dish soap and water
- Adhesive
- Small disposable container
- Grout
- Water

TOOLS

- Apron
- Safety glasses
- Utility knife and/or scissors
- Hard-tipped pen or pencil
- Permanent waterproof fine-tipped
  marker and/or china marker
- Cork-backed straightedge
- Glass cutter
- Tile and/or glass mosaic nippers
- Running pliers
- Breaking/grozing pliers
- Smoothing device – carborundum
  stone, wet/dry sandpaper,
  diamond pad, or glass grinder
- Small containers or jars
- Small palette knife or craft stick
- Tweezers and/or dental tools
- Razor blade and/or paint scraper
- Respirator or dust mask
- Small container for mixing grout
- Rubber or latex gloves
- Sponge
- Soft lint-free cloth
- Soft bristled brushes and/or toothbrush

MOSAIC TERMINOLOGY

ADHERE to attach, cement, fasten, or glue an object to another surface

BURNISH to rub against a surface until smooth and wrinkle-free

BUTTER to apply a thin layer of adhesive to a surface

CEMENT (n) the wet mixture of sand, Portland cement powder, and water (v) to adhere, attach, fasten, or glue an object to another surface

CONCRETE the solid mass that cement becomes once it has hardened and the moisture has evaporated

GRAIN the direction (flow) or arrangement of colors and textures in a sheet of art glass

GROUT (n) cement mixture used to fill interstices (spaces between mosaic pieces) (v) to fill interstices

INTERSTICE the space or gap between adjacent pieces of mosaic material

KEY to abrade or roughen the smooth surface of a base/support structure

SLAKE process where the dry ingredients in a mixture break down and absorb and/or mix with the liquid ingredients

TESSERA(E) the individual piece(s) or unit(s) in a mosaic design

Preparing the Base/Support Structure

1 Clean surface of base/support structure to remove dust, oil, wax, or grease. Glass, glazed ceramic, and other non-porous structures will not require further preparation.

2 Use sandpaper or a carpentry file to smooth surfaces and remove rough edges or burrs on porous structures such as terra-cotta pots and wood boards.

3 Apply an appropriate sealant if necessary. Refer to sidebar/info box About Sealant (p30).

Transferring the Pattern onto a Base/Support Structure

1 Place a sheet of carbon paper over surface area to be covered with tesserae and mosaic pieces. Trim carbon to fit if surface is not flat and fasten with masking tape.

2 Position pattern copy over the carbon and fasten with masking tape in the correct position.

3 Trace pattern with a hard tipped pen or pencil, pressing firmly to transfer design lines onto the base/support structure.

4 If the base/support structure is constructed of wood, key (rough up) the surface, where the mosaic will be placed, by scoring with a utility knife. Small cuts into the wood surface will be sufficient. Do not gouge the wood.

Preparing Mosaic Pieces and Tesserae

1 Cut (pp22,23) quantity and number of uniform and random tesserae as listed for project. Separate tesserae by size and color and store in small jars or containers until ready for use.

2 Use a pattern copy and marker to trace distinctive pattern shapes onto art glass (pp15–16) or other mosaic material.

3 Cut (pp16–22) each piece required, cutting inside the marked pattern line.

4 Smooth and shape pieces to fit within pattern lines and/or to dull sharp and jagged edges (pp24-26). Interstices between tesserae and individual mosaic pieces should be approx. $1/16$ in to $1/8$ in wide to allow for application of grout.

5 Clean each piece with soap and water, rinse, and dry.

6 Apply an appropriate sealant if necessary. Refer to sidebar/info box (p30) About Sealant for specific information.

Adhering Mosaic Pieces and Tesserae to Base/Support Structure

1 Protect areas that will not be covered with tesserae and mosaic materials with masking tape.

2 Choose a ceramic tile adhesive that is appropriate for the project. For outdoor use and mosaics on concrete bases/support structures, use thin-set mortar or water-resistant adhesive containing a latex polymer additive. Read and follow the manufacturer's instructions.

3 If the adhesive color differs from the grout, mix in a bit of grout to tint adhesive a similar shade. Excess adhesive will then be less visible if it oozes from interstices between tesserae and cannot be removed or covered with grout.

4 Most adhesives are pre-mixed and ready for application. Scoop a small amount out of the original container and into a disposable one (e.g. paper cup). Secure lid to adhesive container to prevent air exposure and hardening.

5 Choose a mosaic piece that is part of the main design element or has a distinctive shape. Use a small palette knife or craft stick to butter a thin layer of adhesive onto back of the mosaic piece.

6 Firmly press piece onto base/support structure in the correct position and twist back and forth slightly to embed it in the adhesive. There should be a minimal amount of adhesive oozing from beneath and around bottom edges of the piece.

7 Adhere remaining prominent mosaic pieces to the base/support structure. Applying pieces, color by color, also helps to avoid mistakes in placement.

8 Fill in background of project with remaining tesserae until all areas of the mosaic pattern have been covered. For areas to be filled with quantities of the same shape and size of tessera, save time by applying a layer of adhesive directly onto

Direct Method – The Basic Steps

After verifying pattern fits accurately, transfer pattern onto base/support structure using carbon paper.

The surface of base/support structure must be keyed (roughened) to ensure adhesive will hold the tesserae to the structure.

Adhesive may ooze from beneath the tesserae during application. Mix a bit of grout with adhesive to make oozing less noticeable.

Butter underside of main elements of mosaic design. Press each piece down firmly onto the base/support structure.

Some adhesive may ooze out from beneath the tesserae. Use palette knife to remove any excess adhesive from the tesserae edges.

Once the adhesive has set (approx. 24 hrs), use a razor or scraper point to remove any excess adhesive remaining on top of tesserae.

Grout consistency is important - not too runny, not too stiff. Use gloved hand or damp sponge to work grout into interstices. Wipe the excess grout off mosaic surface.

Let mosaic sit for approximately 40 minutes until a dry haze forms on the surface of the tesserae. Carefully wipe haze off with a soft cloth.

After the grout has cured for 24 hours, buff the mosaic surface with a soft cloth until clean.

base/support structure surface and then pressing the tesserae firmly in place.

9 Use tweezers, dental pick, or utility knife to remove and reposition mosaic pieces and tesserae as necessary.

10 Let adhesive set for 24 hours or as recommended by manufacturer's instructions.

11 Carefully remove any adhesive from the surface of mosaic pieces and tesserae with a paint scraper.

Applying Grout

Select grout that is appropriate in color and texture to complete the project. Determine whether the grout color should compliment or contrast with the mosaic design and the visible portions of the base/ support structure. Non-sanded grouts have a smooth finish and are used for grouting mosaics with narrow interstices between tesserae or easily scratched surfaces. This grout type has a tendency to shrink so additional coats of grout may be necessary to fill in larger spaces or gaps between tesserae. Sanded grout is grittier and can be used for most mosaics, certain outdoor projects, and terra-cotta pots. Choose waterproof or water-resistant grouts and thin-set mortars for finished pieces that are to be left outdoors.

1 In accordance with the manufacturer's instructions, mix required amount of dry grout with cool, clean water until the mixture reaches a stiff, creamy consistency.

2 Let moist grout slake (stand and absorb moisture) for approximately 10 minutes, then re-stir, before applying to the mosaic.

3 Wipe a clean, moist sponge across the surface of the mosaic to slightly dampen tesserae, preventing excessive grout from sticking to their surfaces.

4 With gloved hand or damp sponge apply grout to the mosaic surface. Gently work it between tesserae until grout is flush with the mosaic surface and all crevices are filled.

About Sealant

Do I need to seal the surface of base/ support structures?

Interior settings: Most mosaics adhered to a $^3/_4$ in exterior grade plywood base/support structure do not require sealing. To prevent warping of thinner, more porous wood, seal all sides of the base by brushing on a thin coat of wood sealant or a mixture of 50% all-purpose white glue and 50% water. Permanent installations in bathrooms and kitchens are exposed to more moisture and need site specific treatment.

Exterior settings: Outdoor mosaics should be protected from climate variations by sealing all sides of any wood base/support structure with a silicone-based sealant and using compatible water-resistant adhesives and grout. Use thin-set mortar and grout on concrete surfaces.

Terra-cotta and similar porous materials: Seal the interior of unglazed terra-cotta and pottery containers with water-resistant silicone or put soil and plants in a smaller plastic pot and insert into the container. Store the containers in a dry, protected location during freezing temperatures.

Do I need to use grout sealant?
Use a sealant to protect grout where water-resistance is necessary, such as mosaic tabletops, plant containers, serving trays, etc.

Do I need to seal porous tesserae and mosaic materials?
Apply ceramic tile sealant to the surface of porous materials after cutting and shaping into tesserae and other mosaic shapes. Surfaces of unglazed china and pottery as well as porous substances like marble, limestone, and slate can absorb moisture and expand and may stain or discolor when grouting or handling the project.

Consult tiling or carpentry experts at local hardware stores or home and garden centers for advice if you are unsure if sealant is required for your project and to receive suitable product information.

Methods of Applying Tesserae

Opus refers to the method or style of laying tesserae to form a mosaic.
Andamento is the flow of a mosaic design and is determined by the direction of the tesserae placement and grout lines.

1 OPUS TESSELATUM
Tesserae, similar in size and shape, are applied in horizontal and vertical rows to form an unobtrusive background grid for the main design elements of a mosaic.

2 OPUS REGULATUM
Tesserae of the same shape and size are laid in rows, either vertical or horizontal, similar to the pattern of a brick wall. The tesserae are staggered in each row so that the interstices from one row to the next do not line up to form a grid pattern.

3 OPUS VERMICULATUM
Tesserae are positioned in one or more rows around the perimeter of a larger piece or design element. The tesserae rows outline and accentuate images and lines in the mosaic pattern creating visual interest and depth.

4 OPUS MUSIVUM
An extension of the opus vermiculatum method, continual rows of tesserae are applied, radiating outward from an integral piece or image to the mosaic perimeter. The adamento of the tesserae creates a vibrant design with lots of movement.

5 OPUS SECTILE
Similar in style to a stained glass window, each tessera is cut and configured to a form a specific shape within the overall mosaic design.

6 RANDOM
As the term implies, tesserae of varying shapes and sizes are randomly placed to fill specific areas and/or the background of a mosaic.

5 Use damp sponge to wipe away excess grout and smooth top of grouted areas until level with the mosaic surface.

6 Rinse sponge in cool, clean water, wring out excess, and wipe mosaic surface clean.

7 Allow the grouted mosaic to dry approx. 40 minutes or per the manufacturer's instructions.

8 A dry haze will be apparent on the mosaic surface. Buff haze away with a dry lint-free cloth.

9 Grout requires a minimum of 24 hours to cure. To aid curing process and prevent the grout from drying too quickly and cracking, lightly mist with water several times over the course of the day or cover with a slightly damp cloth or sheet of plastic.

Cleaning the Finished Mosaic

1 Once grout is dry remove any excess by buffing with a soft lint-free cloth and/or a soft bristle brush.

2 Use paint scraper to remove any remaining adhesive or grout still present on the mosaic surface.

3 Remove masking tape used to protect the base/support structure.

4 Apply an appropriate sealant if necessary. Refer to sidebar/info box About Sealant (p30) for specific information.

Finished example of Direct Method Technique

Indirect (Reverse) Method — The Basic Steps

Listed below are the basic materials and tools needed for indirect (reverse) method.

NOTE *Additional listings with specific requirements are provided for each project.*

MATERIALS

- **3 copies of pattern**
- **Base or support structure for mosaic**
- **Sealant (optional)**
- **Masking tape**
- **Clear adhesive-backed vinyl**
- **Newspaper**
- **Mosaic materials for project – art glass, china, tiles, glass nuggets, marbles and jewels, found objects, etc.**
- **Dish soap and water**
- **Adhesive**
- **Cardboard**
- **Clear glass sheet**
- **Flat wood block**
- **Grout**
- **Water**

TOOLS

- **Apron**
- **Safety glasses**
- **Light box (optional)**
- **Permanent waterproof fine-tipped marker and/or china marker**
- **Cork-backed straightedge**
- **Glass cutter**
- **Tile and/or glass mosaic nippers**
- **Running pliers**
- **Breaking/grozing pliers**
- **Smoothing device – carborundum stone, wet/dry sandpaper, diamond pad, or glass grinder**
- **Small containers or jars**
- **Small palette knife or craft stick**
- **Tweezers and/or dental tools**
- **Utility knife and/or scissors**
- **Trowel**
- **Hammer or mallet**
- **Razor blade and/or paint scraper**
- **Respirator or dust mask**
- **Small container for mixing grout**
- **Rubber or latex gloves**
- **Sponge**
- **Soft lint-free cloth**
- **Soft bristle brushes and/or toothbrush**

Preparing the Pattern

1 Make 3 copies (pp14–15) of project pattern.
2 Verify that the outline of the pattern fits within the area on the base or support structure to be covered with tesserae. Compare pattern copies to the original to ensure accuracy. Adjust pattern and/or copies if alterations are required.
3 Use one pattern copy as a guide for cutting, breaking, and shaping mosaic pieces to the correct size and shape (pp16–26). Use second copy to cut out any pattern piece requiring a template (p16) (e.g. for cutting opaque materials) remembering to cut inside pattern lines. The third copy will be placed beneath the clear

adhesive-backed vinyl to guide the placement of tesserae and mosaic pieces.

4 On a light box, place a pattern copy face down and trace the design lines onto the reverse side with permanent marker. If a light box is not available, tape pattern onto a window (with the design facing outward), using daylight to illuminate the lines being traced.

5 Tape the pattern copy to a flat work surface or board, with the reverse side facing upward.

6 Peel the paper backing from a piece of clear adhesive backed vinyl that is approximately $\frac{1}{2}$ in larger on each side than the project pattern. Position the vinyl over the pattern taped to the work surface, with the adhesive side facing up. Do not stick it to the pattern! The vinyl should be centered so that approximately $\frac{1}{2}$ in of vinyl overlaps the pattern on each side. The pattern should be completely covered by the vinyl yet visible through it. Tape in place, taking care not to position tape within the pattern outline.

> **HELPFUL HINTS**
> Use clear 8 mil sandblast resist or mosaic mounting vinyl for the strength of the adhesive and the thickness of the vinyl. These materials are available at most stained glass shops and craft stores. Clear contact paper can be used as an alternative but the adhesive is not as strong and tesserae may not stick as well to its surface.

Preparing the Base/Support Structure

1 Follow the instructions for Preparing the Base/Support Structure as described for the Direct Method (p28).

2 Using the pattern as a guide, mark the outline of the overall mosaic shape onto the base/support structure.

3 If the base/support structure is constructed of wood, key the surface where the mosaic will be placed by scoring with the utility knife. Small cuts into the wood surface will be sufficient. Do not gouge the wood.

Preparing Mosaic Pieces and Tesserae

Follow the instructions for Preparing Mosaic Pieces and Tesserae as described for the Direct Method (p28). Once cut and shaped each piece must be cleaned thoroughly to ensure adhesion to the clear adhesive-backed vinyl.

Placing Mosaic Pieces and Tesserae on Vinyl

The mosaic pieces and tesserae are now ready to be placed onto the clear adhesive-backed vinyl. Remember that the pattern copy under the vinyl is the reverse of the pattern used to cut the pieces.

1 Beginning with the main design elements in the project foreground, turn each piece of the mosaic over and place face down onto the vinyl in the correct position. Press the pieces firmly onto the resist.

2 Fill in background of the project with the remaining tesserae until all areas of the project pattern have been covered.

3 Use tweezers, dental pick, or utility knife to remove and reposition mosaic pieces and tesserae as necessary. Though the ability to shift or replace a piece is an advantage of the indirect method, repeated lifting of pieces from the vinyl can deteriorate the adhesive.

4 Use a utility knife to trim away excess vinyl from the pattern perimeter.

5 For sizable projects, splitting the mosaic piece into several sections will make application to the base/support structure easier. Being careful not to dislodge any pieces, run the knife blade along the interstices between the mosaic pieces, cutting through the vinyl below. Separate into sections as required.

Applying Adhesive

1 Follow steps 1 to 3 from Adhering Mosaic Pieces and Tesserae to Base/Support Structure as described for the Direct Method (p28).

2 Use a notched trowel to apply a thin, even layer of adhesive to the base/support structure where the mosaic is to be applied. Try not to cover the

Indirect (Reverse) Method – The Basic Steps

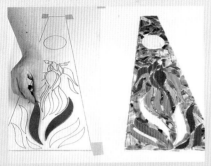

The adhesive-backed vinyl is larger than pattern. Position over pattern, adhesive side up. Tape pattern and vinyl to work surface.

Place the main elements of the mosaic first. Fill in the background last. Trim away excess vinyl when all pieces are down.

For smaller sections, align one edge of mosaic section with corresponding pattern edge. Turn vinyl over and place pieces onto the adhesive.

For ease of handling split large patterns into sections prior to applying to base/support structure.

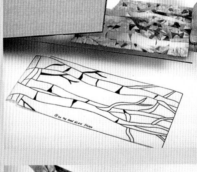

Adhesive is applied with a trowel in the Indirect Method.

For larger sections, sandwich the mosaic between a sheet of glass and cardboard to turn pieces over. Align the mosaic over base and carefully pull the glass sheet from beneath mosaic.

A flat wood block firmly presses glass in place. Allow adhesive to set for 24 hours. Then carefully peel away the vinyl backing.

outside pattern line which acts as the guide for applying the mosaic.

Applying Mosaic to the Base/Support Structure

1 The trick to the indirect method is turning over the sections of mosaic adhered to the vinyl without dislodging the tesserae, then applying each section to the base/support structure in the correct position.

• Smaller mosaic sections can be put in place by following these steps

A With the base/support structure close at hand, gently lift the mosaic-laden vinyl.
B Align one edge of the mosaic section with the corresponding pattern edge.
C Carefully turn the vinyl over and place mosaic pieces onto the adhesive. Check that the mosaic section is correctly positioned and press into place.

• Larger mosaic sections can be accurately applied without dislodging pieces from the vinyl by following these steps

A Carefully slide the mosaic-laden vinyl onto a piece of cardboard and place a clear glass sheet (at least 3mm thick) on top. Both the cardboard and glass sheet must be slightly larger than the mosaic section.
B Hold the layers tightly together and turn the mosaic section over so that the clear glass sheet is now on the bottom. Remove the top cardboard layer.
C Align the mosaic section with two adjacent edges of the glass sheet. Hold the glass sheet over the base/support structure and line up the edges of the mosaic section with the area where it is to be applied. The glass sheet must not touch the adhesive.
D Grasp the edges of the vinyl. With the aid of a helper, pull the clear glass sheet out from beneath the mosaic section. Press the mosaic firmly to the adhesive.

E Repeat steps A to D for each mosaic section to be adhered. Align sections so that a visible seam or division is not apparent between them – the mosaic should look like one unit, not a series of ill-fitting sections.

2 Do not remove the vinyl at this stage. Pieces may come away with the vinyl if it is peeled off before the adhesive has set.
3 Use a flat wood block and a hammer or mallet to gently tamp mosaic sections down onto the adhesive until firmly in place.
4 Let the adhesive set for 24 hours or as recommended by manufacturer's instructions.
5 Remove the vinyl, exposing the top side of the mosaic.
6 Carefully remove any adhesive from the surface of mosaic pieces and tesserae with a new razor blade or paint scraper.

Applying Grout and Cleaning the Finished Mosaic

Follow the same instructions for these final stages as described for the Direct Method (pp30,31).

Base/Support Structures

Many everyday objects can be revitalized and turned into objects d'art with the artistic application of mosaic designs and materials. Furniture pieces, picture frames, ceramic or glass vessels, and birdbaths are examples of items that can serve as a base/support structure if the surface is relatively smooth, the structure can bear the weight of the tesserae, and an appropriate adhesive is used to secure the mosaic. Specific information and requirements for the preparation of base/support structures are described in the instructions given for each project.

Making Wood Base/Support Structures for Mosaics

Mosaic projects are often fabricated on wood base/support structures to create eclectic wall hangings, cabinet panels, mirrors, furniture, and more. Patterns can be adjusted to suit ready-made base/support structures or you can make the base from plywood. Due to strength and durability, $^3/_4$ in exterior grade plywood is recommended for making a base/support structure that will support the weight of a mosaic and will rarely warp. If you do not have the necessary woodworking skills and tools, enlist a friend who does to assist or make the base/support structure for you. When operating power tools, read the manufacturer's directions and follow all safety guidelines and precautions. Always wear an apron and safety glasses.

MATERIALS

- **1 copy of pattern**
- **$^3/_4$ in exterior grade plywood**
- **Wood trim molding (at least $^1/_4$ in wide)**
- **Carpenter's wood glue**
- **Finishing nails**
- **Wood filler**
- **Sandpaper**
- **Wood stain or paint**
- **Felt or cork pads**

TOOLS

- **Apron**
- **Safety glasses**
- **Marking pen or pencil**
- **Drawing or carpenter's square**
- **Wood saw (hand or power)**
- **Hammer or air nailer**
- **Applicator brush for wood stain or paint**
- **Soft cloths for buffing**

Instructions

1 Measure the width and height of the project pattern.

2 Trace the outline of the base onto the plywood sheet with a marking pen or pencil. Use a square and straightedge when drawing the dimensions of square or rectangular base/support structures to ensure that corners are the correct angle.

3 Cut the base piece away from the sheet of plywood, using a wood saw.

4 For straight-sided projects requiring a raised edge, cut a length of wood trim molding for each of the sides of the base piece. Each end must be mitered at the appropriate angle to give the corners of the base a finished appearance (miter each end of the molding for square and

rectangular projects at a 45° angle).

5 Apply a bead of carpenter's wood glue to an outside edge of base piece and place a length of molding overtop. Fasten molding to base pieces with a hammer and finishing nails. Repeat this step with remaining lengths of trim, making sure mitered ends of each length are butted up against the adjacent pieces. Wood trim should be slightly wider than base piece so a raised edge is present around the perimeter of base piece. The raised edge will contain mosaic tesserae so they do not protrude over the edge and will give the base a finished and professional appearance.

6 Fill nail holes and gaps with wood filler and smooth with sandpaper.

7 The base/support structure can be painted or stained before or after the mosaic has been adhered to the base and the project has been grouted. Choose a stain or paint complementary to the grout color and the mosaic materials. Do not paint or stain any surface that will be covered with mosaic tesserae.

8 Apply felt or cork pads to back of base piece to prevent marring of wall or furniture surfaces.

Mounting Mosaic Wall Pieces

Mosaic wall hangings and mirrors can be hung, like any other type of picture or wall decoration.

1 Place the wall hanging or mirror face down on to the work surface.

2 Make two opposing marks 4 in from the top of the base and $1^{1}/_{2}$ in to 2 in from either side.

3 Fasten a heavy-duty eyelet hanger or an eye screw to plywood base at each mark. Use screws that are approximately $^{1}/_{2}$ in in length so they will not penetrate through the $^{3}/_{4}$ in plywood and damage the mosaic on the front.

4 String a double strand of picture hanging wire between the two hangers, threading it through the eyes. Wrap the ends of the wire around the strand several times to secure.

5 Hang small mosaic pieces directly on the wall on a picture hook or small nail. To hang larger and heavier pieces, drill two holes into the wall in desired location. Insert appropriate plugs or anchors, depending on the type of wall surface. Insert and tighten a screw three quarters of the way into each plug. Suspend mosaic piece on the wall by hooking the wire onto the two screws.

Care and Maintenance of Finished Mosaic Projects

Many of the mosaics featured in this book are meant for display in the home. The finished projects require occasional dusting and can be cleaned by wiping with a cloth dampened with water or a light spray of ammonia-free window cleaner. Lightly buff the mosaic surface dry with a soft lint-free cloth. Grouted areas can be made more resistant to stains and moisture by applying a grout sealant. See About Sealant (p30) for more information.

The Serenity birdbath (p57), the Phoenix Rising garden marker (p92), and the Garden Stone projects (p110) are designed for outdoor use. Thin-set mortar, latex polymer additives, and concrete are used in place of tile adhesives and grouts to give the projects the additional strength and protection necessary for exposure to the elements. Mosaic surfaces can be cleaned by lightly brushing with a mild dish soap and water. A few drops of bleach can be added to the water to help remove stubborn stains. Rinse projects thoroughly with clean water and buff dry with a soft lint-free cloth. Birdbaths should be cleaned on a weekly basis and fresh water supplied for the birds. Store the projects indoors during periods of extreme weather. Inclement conditions, such as freezing and thawing, snow, or hail have the potential to break or crack glass pieces and other mosaic materials.

All projects can be repaired or touched up if tesserae or grout comes loose from the mosaic surface by using appropriate materials and following directions that relate to the situation. It is usually a matter of applying adhesive and reinserting the tesserae into the mosaic and re-grouting the surrounding area.

Mosaic Projects and Patterns

Baby's First ABCs
Wall Plaques

Letter height $6^{1}/_{4}$ in

MOSAIC MATERIAL REQUIRED
Letter A
16 – $^{3}/_{4}$ in x $^{3}/_{4}$ in rose pink vitreous glass mosaic tiles
Letter B
20 – $^{3}/_{4}$ in x $^{3}/_{4}$ in robin egg blue vitreous glass mosaic tiles
Letter C
18 – $^{3}/_{4}$ in x $^{3}/_{4}$ in spring green vitreous glass mosaic tiles
Letters refer to type and quantity of mosaic material used for this project. The quantities and types listed are the minimum requirements for completing this project as illustrated, but materials may be substituted and quantities modified as necessary.
NOTE *There is no pattern for this mosaic project.*

Specific and/or Additional Materials and Tools Required

MATERIALS
Precut wood letters A, B, C
Ivory sanded grout
Pale yellow latex paint

Base/Support Structure

Pre-cut letters of the alphabet are available in a wide variety of fonts and sizes and can be purchased at craft and hardware stores. The letters are a perfect size to work with while practicing mosaic techniques before tackling larger projects. To make your own letters refer to Base/Support Structures (p35) for basic guidelines. The letters were painted with pale yellow latex paint before the vitreous glass tiles were applied.

Mosaic Instructions

Construct the mosaics applied to the face of the letters by following the instructions given for Direct Method (pp26–31). Refer to the photograph of the finished letters as a guide for tesserae placement.

• $^{3}/_{4}$ in x $^{3}/_{4}$ in squares cut from comparable shades of art glass can be used as a substitute for vitreous glass mosaic tiles.
• Refer to Mounting Mosaic Wall Pieces (p37) for instructions on hanging the finished mosaic.

Shining Stars
Wall Clock and Plaques

Specific and/or Additional Materials and Tools Required

MATERIALS
24 in x 28 in piece of $^3/_4$ in exterior grade plywood
Clock movement with 1 in long shaft
Ocean blue sanded grout

TOOLS
Jigsaw
Power drill with $^3/_4$ in bit

Base/Support Structure

Guidelines for constructing the bases are given in Making Wood Base/Support Structures for Mosaics (pp36,37). Specific instructions for this project are as follows:

1 Trace outlines of star shapes onto the sheet of plywood.

2 Using a jigsaw, cut out the base shapes along the traced outlines.

3 Sand all edges smooth with sandpaper.

4 Key (score) plywood surfaces with a utility knife to aid adhesion.

5 Drill a hole through the large plywood star in the position marked on the pattern.

Mosaic Instructions

Construct the star wall clock and plaques by following the instructions given for the Direct Method (p26–31). Refer to the photograph of the finished mosaics as a guide for tesserae placement. The accompanying instructions are particular to fabricating the wall clock. Instructions specific to this project are as follows:

1 Fit the shaft movement of the clock through the hole. Verify that clock hands will be able to move freely and there is enough space to accommodate the addition of mirrored tesserae and glass moon face

and stars. Set clock movement aside until mosaic portion of project is complete.

2 Adhere the glass stars (D) and glass moon face (C) to the large star base/support structure in the 3, 6, 9, and 12 o'clock positions.

3 Apply random-size tesserae (A, B) to face of star-shaped base until surface is entirely covered. Ensure that tesserae do not protrude past the edge of the base and that a $^1/_{16}$ in space is left free of tesserae around perimeter of hole drilled for the clock movement.

4 With the base lying flat on work surface, glue tesserae (A, B) along the outside edge of the plywood, approx. $^1/_{16}$ in apart. Cut (p23) a tessera to fit any space that will not accommodate a whole piece.

5 Once the adhesive has cured (approximately 24 hours), follow the instructions for Applying Grout (pp30–31) and Cleaning Finished Piece (p31).

6 Fasten the clock movement to the finished mosaic (see the manufacturer's instructions).

7 Refer to Mounting Mosaic Wall Pieces (p37) for instructions on hanging the finished mosaic.

8 To make the small and medium star plaques skip steps 1, 2, and 6 that pertain to the addition of the clock movement.

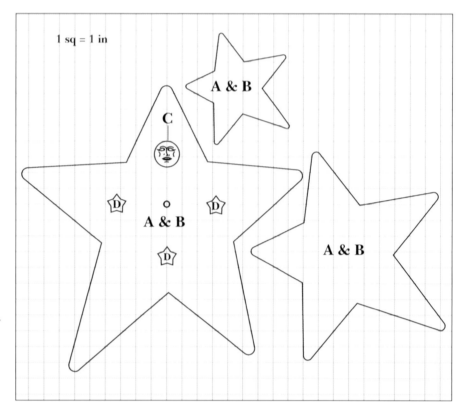

1 sq = 1 in

A & B

C

A & B

D

D

D

A & B

Verify that clock hands can move freely without touching the glass moon face and stars before applying tesserae.

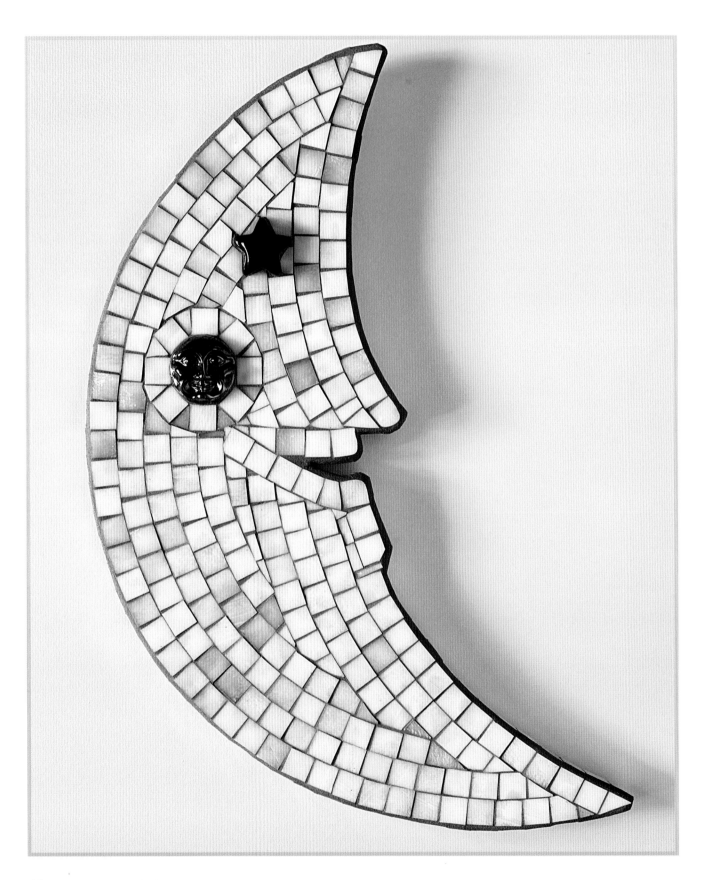

Man in the Moon
Wall Hanging

MOSAIC PANEL DIMENSIONS

18 in high x 13⁵/₈ in wide

MOSAIC MATERIAL REQUIRED

A 1 dark blue glass star

B 1 iridescent dark blue glass moon face

C 12 in x 24 in iridescent white ring mottle art glass

Letters refer to type and quantity of mosaic material used for pattern on page 46. The quantities and types listed are the minimum requirements for completing this project as illustrated, but materials may be substituted and quantities modified as necessary.

Specific and/or Additional Materials and Tools Required

MATERIALS
Ocean blue sanded grout

20 in x 16 in piece of ³/₄ in exterior grade plywood

TOOLS
Jigsaw

Base/Support Structure
Guidelines for constructing a base are given in Making Wood Base/Support Structures for Mosaics (pp36-37). Specific instructions for this project are as follows:

1 Trace the Man in the Moon outline on a sheet of plywood.

2 Using a jigsaw, cut out base shape along traced outline.

3 Smooth edges with sandpaper.

4 Key (score) the plywood surface with a utility knife to aid adhesion.

Mosaic Instructions
Construct project by following instructions given for Direct Method (pp26–31). Refer to photo of finished mosaic as a guide for tesserae placement. Instructions specific to this project are as follows:

1 Cut a 12 in x 4 in piece of the iridescent white ring mottle art glass (C) into ³/₄ in x ³/₄ in square tesserae to be applied along the outside of the base. Cut the remainder of the glass sheet into ⁵/₈ in x ⁵/₈ in square tesserae that will be used to create the mosaic on the front surface of the base.

2 Use a pattern copy to determine the correct position of the glass star (A) and the glass moon face (B). Glue the two glass shapes to the base using tile adhesive.

3 Adhere eight – ⁵/₈ in x ⁵/₈ in tesserae in a circular row around glass moon face. Use a glass cutter to trim tesserae to fit into small triangular interstices along the perimeter of the circle and glue in place.

4 The opus vermiculatum (p31) style of mosaic design is used to determine the position that the ⁵/₈ in tesserae are adhered to base. Beginning at the tip of the moon, apply a row of tesserae along inner curve of base to the tip of the nose. The interstices between tesserae should be approx. ¹/₁₆ in. Use a glass cutter or mosaic nippers to trim tesserae as required to fit outline of base and to fill spaces not large enough to accommodate a

whole piece. Ensure that the tesserae do not protrude past the edge of the base.

5 Apply a row of tesserae following the contour of lower lip, continuing until tesserae row around the glass moon face is reached. Next, adhere tesserae along edge of upper lip and then apply a row following the shape of the chin from lower lip to the bottom tip of the base. One long continuous row of tesserae is applied to remaining outer curve to completely outline the shape of the Man in the Moon base.

6 Start a new row within the one just completed. Once row is glued begin a new row on opposite side. Working towards center, fill in the remainder of the mosaic by adhering the rows in the same manner. Trim each tessera to fit into the spaces not large enough to accommodate a whole piece.

7 Lay the base flat on the work surface, adhere $^3/_4$ in x $^3/_4$ in tesserae along the outside edge of the plywood, approximately $^1/_{16}$ in apart.

8 Once the adhesive has cured (approximately 24 hours), follow the instructions for Applying Grout (pp30–31) and Cleaning Finished Piece (p30).

9 Refer to Mounting Mosaic Wall Pieces (p37) for the instructions on hanging the finished mosaic. The irregular shape of the Man in the Moon allows the wall hanging to be hung at any angle.

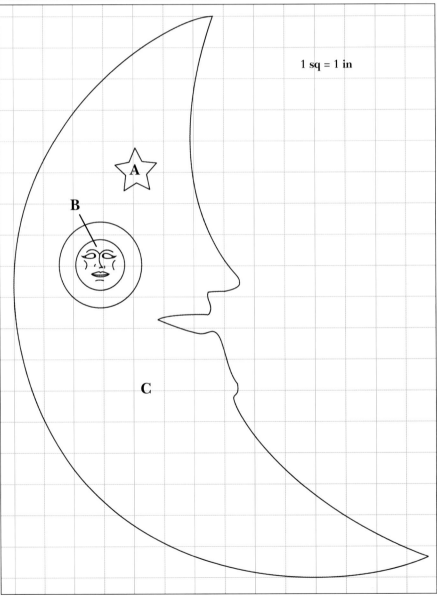

1 sq = 1 in

Bonsai
Tea Tray

MOSAIC PANEL DIMENSIONS
12 in high x 18 in wide

MOSAIC MATERIAL REQUIRED

A 8 in x 8 in gold iridescent black art glass

B 6 in x 6 in iridescent red with white wispy art glass

C 6 in x 8 in textured green with brown and white wispy art glass

D 6 in x 6 in dark brown art glass

E 8 in x 8 in gray and burgundy wispy art glass (cut into $^3/_4$ in x $^3/_4$ in tesserae)

F 8 in x 8 in medium blue and white wispy art glass (cut into random-size tesserae)

G 8 in x 8 in dark blue and white wispy art glass (cut into random-size tesserae)

Letters refer to type and quantity of art glass used for pattern on page 49. The quantities and types listed are the minimum requirements for completing this project as illustrated, but materials may be substituted and quantities modified as necessary.

Specific and/or Additional Materials and Tools Required

MATERIALS

Black sanded grout
Heavy-duty masking tape
  (optional)
Glass etching cream
  (optional)
12 in x 18 in sheet of 6mm
  clear glass (optional)
4 acrylic bumper pads
  (optional)

Base/Support Structure

• Wood tray with a recessed area measuring 12 in x 18 in. A pre-fabricated wood tray is the base/support structure for this mosaic project. Adjust pattern as necessary if dimensions of your tray differ.

Mosaic Instructions

The mosaic panel can be made using either the Direct Method (pp26–31) or the Indirect (Reverse) Method (pp32–35) of mosaic construction. Choose method you prefer. Refer to photo of finished mosaic as a guide for tesserae placement. Instructions specific to this project are as follows:

1 Cut (pp16–23) and shape (pp24–26) all the required tesserae as shown on the pattern (p49). Lay foliage pieces (C) in the mosaic with textured side facing upwards.

Remember to reverse the pattern when tracing shapes onto the smooth side of the glass for cutting.

2 Surface of sun (B) is etched with the Japanese symbol for happiness. To achieve this effect, follow these steps:
• Cover top surface of glass piece with masking tape.
• Trace symbol on masking tape as shown on the pattern.
• Use utility knife (with a fresh blade) to cut masking tape along traced lines, taking care not to press too hard and scoring the glass surface below. Remove the cut masking tape, revealing glass surface below. The exposed surface can be lightly sandblasted to reveal symbol. If you do not have sandblasting equipment, use glass etching cream available at craft and/or hardware stores. Follow the manufacturer's instructions and apply etching cream to glass surface. When ready, wash the cream away and remove the masking tape, unveiling the symbol below.

3 Lay down the four corners (A) and the $^3/_4$ in x $^3/_4$ in border pieces (E) and then continue with the specific shapes representing the container (A), the sun (B), the tree foliage (C), and the tree limbs (D). Fill in background area

of the mosaic with random-size tesserae (F, G).

4 Allow the adhesive to set for 24 hours

5 Follow the instructions for Applying Grout (pp30–31) and Cleaning Finished the Piece (p31).

6 Apply a grout sealant (p30) especially if tray will be used for serving food. A sheet of clear glass set over the mosaic will offer further protection from spills and supply an even surface for china. Attach acrylic bumper pads to underside corners of the glass sheet to keep it in place and prevent the glass from rattling against the mosaic.

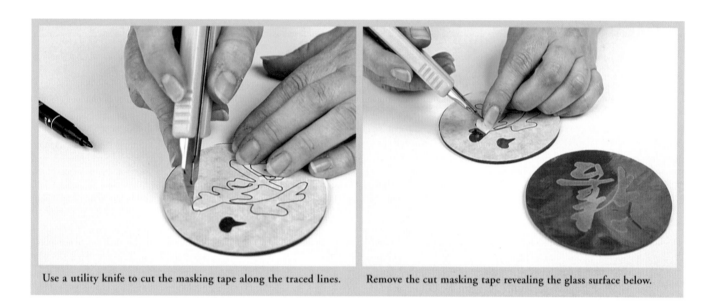

Use a utility knife to cut the masking tape along the traced lines.

Remove the cut masking tape revealing the glass surface below.

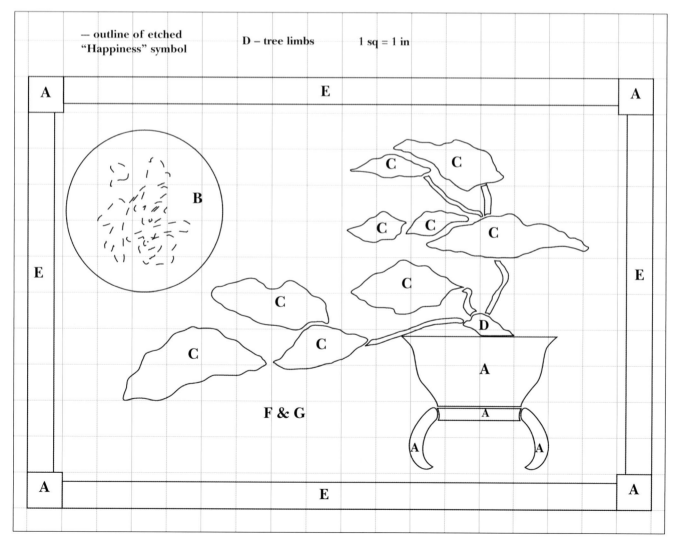

— outline of etched
"Happiness" symbol

D – tree limbs

1 sq = 1 in

Rocky Raccoon
Wall Hanging

MOSAIC PANEL DIMENSIONS
18 in high x 18 in wide

MOSAIC MATERIAL REQUIRED
A 12 in x 12 in white art glass
B 12 in x 12 in black art glass
C 12 in x 10 in mirrored & textured clear art glass
D 5 in x 5 in opaque orange and white wispy art glass
E 14 in x 14 in mirrored dark blue art glass (cut into random-size tesserae)
F 14 in x 14 in rippled dark translucent blue art glass (cut into random-size tesserae)
G 2 iridescent opaque white glass nuggets (medium)
H 1 black glass nugget
Letters refer to type and quantity of mosaic material used for pattern on p 52. The quantities and types listed are the minimum requirements for completing this project as illustrated, but materials may be substituted and quantities modified as necessary.

Specific and/or Additional Materials and Tools Required

MATERIALS
Black sanded grout
Clear silicone adhesive

Base/Support Structure
• 1 piece 18 in x 18 in of ³/₄ in exterior grade plywood with wood trim moldings around the outside edge. Guidelines for constructing a base with wood trim molding are given in Making Wood Base/Support Structures for Mosaics (pp36–37).

Mosaic Instructions
Construct mosaic panel by following instructions given for the Direct Method (pp26–31). Refer to photo of the finished mosaic as a guide for tesserae placement. Instructions specific to this project are as follows:
1 Cut (pp16–23) and shape (pp24–26) all required tesserae as indicated on pattern (p52).
2 Begin by placing and adhering to the base, pieces cut to form shapes representing the raccoon (A, B, H), water ripples (C), and fish tail (D).
3 Fill in remaining open areas of the mosaic with random-size tesserae (E, F) to finish water background. Position tesserae cut from mirrored dark blue

art glass (F) with textured side facing upwards. Allow 24 hours for adhesive to set.
4 Follow instructions for Applying Grout (pp30–31) and Cleaning Finished Piece (p31).
5 Once grout has set and project is clean, 2 white glass nuggets (G) are adhered to mosaic to form the raccoon's eyes. Use the pattern as a guide, put a dab of silicone on underside of each glass nugget and glue them onto surface of corresponding glass pieces. Let silicone set for 24 hours until nuggets are secured.
6 Refer to Mounting Mosaic Wall Pieces (p37) for the instructions on hanging the finished mosaic.

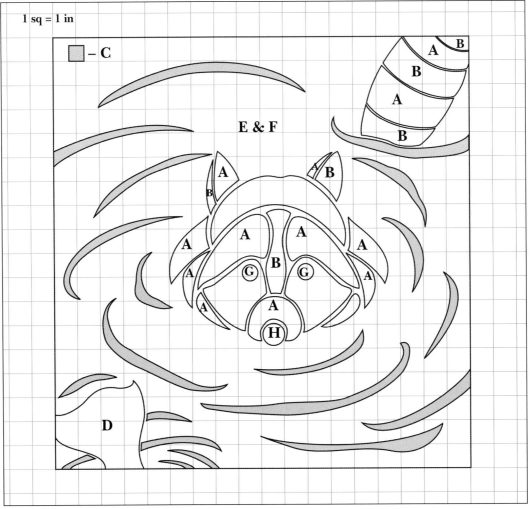

1 sq = 1 in

☐ – C

B
A
B
A
B

E & F

A
B

A B

A
A
A

A
A

A
B
G
G
A

A
A

A
H

D

Dream
Wall Hanging

MOSAIC PANEL DIMENSIONS

10¹/₂ in high x 30 in wide

MOSAIC MATERIAL REQUIRED

A   16 in x 18 in clear, white, gold-pink, and purple art glass
(cut 12 in x 12 in into ¹/₂ in x ³/₄ in tesserae; cut remainder into
random-size tesserae)

B   12 in x 12 in mixed blues ring mottle art glass (cut into ¹/₂ in x ¹/₂ in tesserae)

C   12 in x 12 in mixed purples ring mottle art glass (cut into ¹/₂ in x ¹/₂ in tesserae)

D   3 in x 3 in mirrored dark blue semi-antique art glass (cut into ¹/₂ in x ¹/₂ in tesserae)

E   3 in x 3 in 3mm mirror (cut into ¹/₂ in x ¹/₂ in tesserae)

F   1 iridescent clear glass moon face

G   2 large clear glass stars

H   3 small clear glass stars

Letters refer to type and quantity of mosaic material used for pattern on page 56. The
quantities and types listed are the minimum requirements for completing this project as
illustrated, but materials may be substituted and quantities modified as necessary.

Specific and/or Additional Materials and Tools Required

MATERIALS

20 in x 30 in piece of $^3/_4$ in
   exterior grade plywood
Wood trim moldings
Carpenter's glue
12 – #8 wood screws
   (1 in long)
6 in x 6 in piece of adhesive-
   backed aluminum foil
Charcoal sanded grout

TOOLS

Jigsaw
Power drill

Base/Support Structure

Guidelines for constructing a base are given in Making Wood Base/Support Structures for Mosaics (pp36–37). Specific instructions for this project are as follows:

1 Cut a 10$^1/_2$ in x 30 in main base piece from the larger sheet of plywood. Attach wood moldings around the perimeter of the base.

2 Trace the mosaic pattern onto the main base piece.

3 Trace outlines of the letter D and the 4 connected letters onto the sheet of plywood.

4 Using a jigsaw cut out letters along the traced outlines.

5 Sand the edges of the letters with sandpaper until smooth.

6 Key (score) surfaces of letters and the main base piece with a utility knife to aid adhesion.

7 Attach the letters to the base/support structure. Spread a thin layer of carpenter's glue on the underside of the letters and apply them to the main base piece. Use a power drill to fasten the letters securely to the base with wood screws, countersinking the screws until they are flush with the plywood surface.

Mosaic Instructions

Construct the mosaic panel by following the instructions given for the Direct Method (pp26–31). Refer to the photograph of the finished mosaic as a guide for tesserae placement. Instructions specific to this project are as follows:

1 Cut (pp16–23) and shape (pp24–26) all required tesserae as indicated on pattern (p56).

2 Glue the clear glass moon face (F) and stars (G, H) to the main base piece. To add sparkle and obscure the adhesive beneath the glass, cover the underside of the shapes with an adhesive-backed aluminum foil before gluing.

• Wash the moon face and stars with soap and water to remove traces of oil or grease and any dirt that may be stuck to their surfaces. Buff dry with a lint-free cloth.

• Cut a piece of adhesive-backed foil just large enough to cover a single glass shape. Peel away the waxed paper backing, position the foil over the underside of the glass piece, and press the foil firmly to its surface. Burnish (rub back and forth) the foil to the glass, smoothing away any wrinkles in the foil.

• Place the foiled side of the glass shape down on the work surface. Use a utility knife (with a fresh blade) to cut along the outside edge of the shape and remove excess foil.

3 Begin filling in the background sky located in the upper portion of the mosaic panel. Align a row of the blue tesserae (B) along the top of the curving line drawn on the base. This line acts as a guide for the andamento (flow) of the tesserae, resulting in undulating rows radiating towards the upper edge of the mosaic. This style of mosaic application is referred to as opus musivum (p31). Use a glass cutter or mosaic nippers to trim tesserae as required to fill spaces not large enough to accommodate a whole piece and to fit around the outline of the letters, moon face, and stars. Intermingle several mirror pieces (D) throughout the sky to emulate stars.

4 Continue by filling in the lower portion of the sky with purple tesserae (C), interspersing the remaining mirrored tesserae (D) throughout. Apply the first row beneath the curved bottom row

of tesserae already adhered and keep on laying row after row, working your way to the bottom of the mosaic panel until the base has been completely covered with tesserae.

5 Begin placing and gluing the tesserae to the letters that form the word "Dream". Adhere the random-size tesserae (A) to the face of the letters until the surface is entirely covered. Ensure that the tesserae do not protrude past the edge of the plywood base. Intermingle several mirror pieces (E) throughout the letters to add visual interest.

6 Apply the $^{1}/_{2}$ in x $^{1}/_{2}$ in tesserae (A) along the outside edges of the letters, trimming a tessera as necessary to fit into spaces that are not large enough to accommodate a whole piece. The bottom edge of the tesserae will rest on tesserae adhered to the base. Set the project aside for approximately 24 hours to allow the adhesive to set.

7 Follow the instructions for Applying Grout (pp30–31) and Cleaning the Finished Piece (p31).

8 Refer to Mounting Mosaic Wall Pieces (p37) for instructions on hanging the finished mosaic.

Apply carpenter's glue to underside of letters and press them to the main base

Stages of foil application to back of glass stars

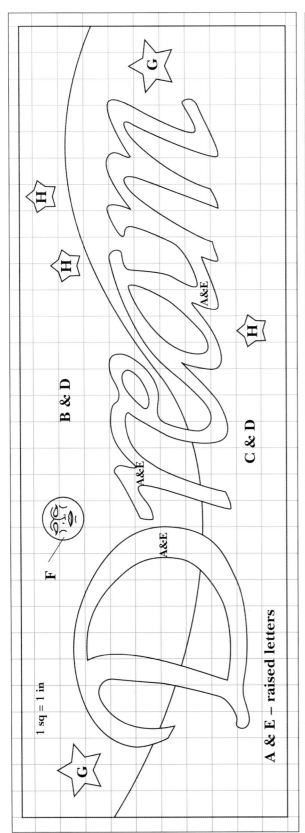

1 sq = 1 in

F

B & D

A&E

A&E

A&E

A&E

G

H

H

H

G

C & D

A & E – raised letters

Serenity
Birdbath

Specific and/or Additional Materials and Tools Required

MATERIALS

14 in terra cotta basin with glazed interior and metal base
Thin-set mortar
Liquid latex polymer additive (optional)

Base/Support Structure

Ready-made birdbaths are available in a variety of styles at home and garden centers as well as craft, department, and hardware stores. The birdbath used for this project consists of a terra cotta basin with a glazed ceramic interior and an accompanying metal stand. The ceramic glaze prevents water in the basin from being absorbed by the terra cotta thus leaving an ample supply for the birds. Upon completion of mosaic, the basin is placed upon the stand or can be hung from chains and displayed in the garden.

Mosaic Instructions

The mosaic is constructed by following instructions given for Direct Method (pp26–31). Refer to photo of finished birdbath as a guide for tesserae placement. Instructions specific to this project are as follows:

1 Select 3 to 4 rocks and/or shells to fit into the space of grouping (D) on the pattern.

2 Cut (pp16–23) and shape (pp24–26) mirrored art glass pieces (B, C) as on the pattern.

3 Referring to Cutting and Shaping Tesserae and Other Mosaic Materials (pp23–24), cut and shape china (A) into smaller pieces. A white china vase with a blue pattern was used for this birdbath. Place vase in a sturdy bag and hit with a hammer to break it. Use glass mosaic cutters or nippers to shape the china fragments into smaller, flatter pieces.

4 Thin-set mortar is used for both adhering and grouting china fragments and glass shapes to the bottom and inner sides of the basin. Prepare enough mortar to cover inside surface of basin. Add dry mortar mix to water and mix to a thick, smooth, creamy consistency. Allow mixture to sit and slake for 10 minutes. Manufacturer's directions give exact ingredients and measurements. For added

bond strength and water resistance, use a liquid latex polymer additive in place of water.

5 With a small trowel or rubber spatula, spread layer of mortar mix ($\frac{1}{16}$ in to $\frac{1}{8}$ in thick) over the bottom of the basin.

6 Apply rocks and/or shells (D), mirrored art glass shapes (B, C), and glass nuggets (E, F) to mortar-covered surface in positions indicated on pattern. Slightly embed pieces into the mortar. There should be a minimal amount of oozing.

7 Start applying china fragments to the mortar. Lay pieces around perimeter of the rock/shell formation and then continue working in rows radiating outwards to rim of basin. Cutting and shaping of china pieces to accommodate the mirrored art glass and glass nuggets or slight shifting of glass shapes may be required. Butter (p27) back of pieces with more mortar to fill any small spaces. Effect of water rippling away from rock/shell formation will become evident. The andamento (p31) of the mosaic background pieces and style of application is known as opus musivum (p31).

8 Once bottom of basin is covered, apply a layer of thin-set mortar to inner rim and apply china pieces in rows around perimeter until lip of basin is reached. Leave top outer lip free of mortar and china fragments.

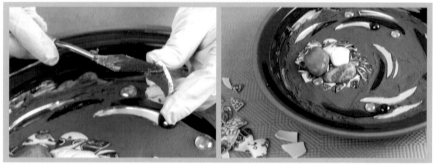

9 Immediately wipe excess mortar from the face of glass shapes and china pieces with a water-dampened sponge.

10 Allow mortar to cure for 24 hours.

11 Mix a fresh batch of thin-set mortar and follow instructions for Applying Grout (pp30–31) to fill interstices between mosaic pieces. Let mortar set for 24 hours before Cleaning Finished Piece (p31).

12 Allow mortar to cure for several days. Place birdbath in garden and filling with water.

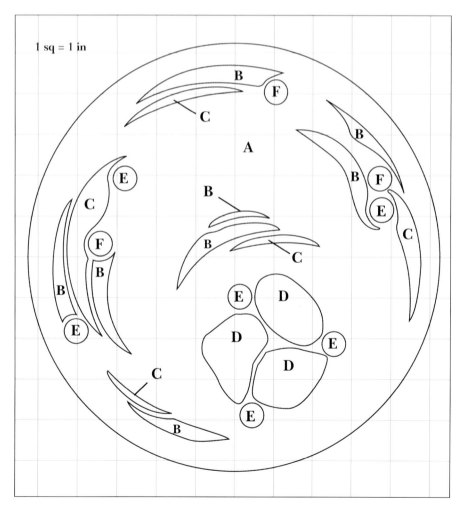

1 sq = 1 in

MOSAIC PANEL DIMENSIONS

3 panels 29¹/₂ in high x 15¹/₂ in wide

MOSAIC MATERIAL REQUIRED

A   16 in x 16 in opaque red and white streaky art glass

B   20 in x 20 in mirrored water-textured copper art glass

C   12 in x 16 in mirrored granite-textured clear art glass

D   8 in x 12 in opaque medium brown and white wispy art glass

E   8 in x 12 in opaque dark brown and white wispy art glass

F   16 in x 24 in granite-textured opaque sage green and white wispy art glass

G   24 in x 24 in iridescent opaque amber and white streaky art glass

H   20 in x 24 in opaque lilac and white wispy art glass

J   12 in x 12 in granite-textured iridescent blues, yellow, and gold-pink streaky art glass

NOTE *The letter I is not used in this listing*

Letters refer to type and quantity of mosaic material used for pattern on page 62. The quantities and types listed are the minimum requirements for completing this project as illustrated, but materials may be substituted and quantities modified as necessary.

Prairie Vista Triptych
Wall Hangings

Specific and/or Additional Materials and Tools Required

MATERIALS
Black sanded grout

Base/Support Structure
• 3 pieces 29$\frac{1}{2}$ in x 15$\frac{1}{2}$ in of $\frac{3}{4}$ in exterior grade plywood with wood trim moldings around the outside edge Guidelines for constructing a base with wood trim molding are given in Making Wood Base/Support Structures for Mosaics (pp36–37).

Mosaic Instructions
Construct each of the three mosaic panels by following instructions given for Direct Method (pp26–31). Refer to photo of the finished mosaics as a guide for tesserae placement. Instructions specific to this project are as follows:
1 Cut (pp16–23) and shape (pp24–26) all tesserae as indicated on patterns.
• Pieces cut from art glass selection F and J are adhered to the base/support structure with textured underside turned upwards. Turn pattern over and trace the reverse image of the pattern shapes onto the smooth top surface of the glass sheet to be cut.
2 Opus sectile (p31) is used for this project. The individual pieces are cut, shaped, and laid out like a stained glass window. Adhere largest pieces to the base/support structure first and then complete mosaic design by attaching the remaining smaller tesserae. Allow the adhesive to set 24 hours.
3 The heads of wheat are accentuated by slightly wider interstices (spaces) between the wheat and the pieces adjacent to them. These wider interstices are filled with grout. Follow the instructions for Applying Grout (pp30–31) and Cleaning the Finished Piece (p31).
4 Refer to Mounting Mosaic Wall Pieces (p37) for the instructions on hanging the finished mosaics.

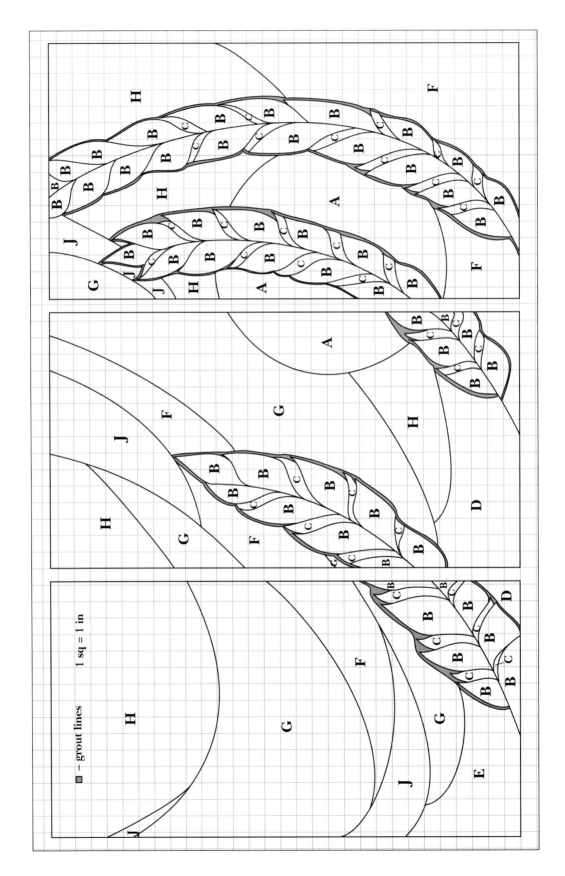

Birch Grove
Cabinet Door Panel

MOSAIC PANEL DIMENSIONS
44 in high x 14 in wide

MOSAIC MATERIAL REQUIRED

A 12 in x 20 in white, brown, and gray opal art glass

B 12 in x 12 in translucent dark gray semi-antique art glass

C 14 in x 20 in blue and white with green and brown fractures art glass
(cut into random-size square and rectangular tesserae no larger than 1 in x 1 in)

D 12 in x 16 in cobalt and white with green and brown fractures art glass
(D1 – cut into random-size square and rectangular tesserae no larger than 1 in x 1 in;
D2 – cut into small random-size tesserae)

E 6 in x 8 in light green and blue fractures art glass (cut into random-size tesserae)

F 6 in x 6 in green and streaky ring mottle art glass (cut into random-size tesserae)

G 14 in x 18 in sky blue and white wispy with rose pink art glass

H small polished stones to cover an area approximately 1 in x 6 in

J 4 in x 4 in emerald, spring, and light green ring mottle art glass

K 6 in x 3 in blue, emerald green, and white ring mottle art glass

L 4 in x 2 in purple, emerald green, and white ring mottle art glass

M 4 in x 4 in medium green and amber streaky art glass

N 4 in x 4 in green and brown with brown streamers art glass

P 5 in x 5 in green and amber with multi-colored fractures art glass

Q 4 in x 6 in spring and dark green and amber streaky art glass

R 6 in x 7 in white ring mottle art glass

NOTE *The letters I and O are not used in this listing*

Letters refer to type and quantity of art glass used for pattern on page 66. The quantities and types listed are the minimum requirements for completing this project as illustrated, but materials may be substituted and quantities modified as necessary.

Specific and/or Additional Materials and Tools Required

MATERIALS
Gray sanded grout

Base/Support Structure
The mosaic panel for this project was applied to an existing 46 in x 16 in cabinet door panel.

• Lightly abrade smooth varnished or painted surfaces with sandpaper to provide "tooth" for the adhesive to stick to.

• Fasten wood trim moldings around the door panel perimeter to provide a finished edge for the mosaic.

• Adjust the pattern as necessary to fit dimensions and configurations of cabinet door panel chosen for your project. Guidelines for constructing a base with wood trim molding are given in Making Wood Base/Support Structures for Mosaics (pp36–37).

Mosaic Instructions
To expedite the mosaic process, construct the panel using the Indirect (Reverse) Method (pp32–35). By assembling the panel on clear adhesive-backed vinyl, less time and effort will be spent gluing the mosaic to the base/support structure. However, the Direct Method (pp26–31) can be used if that is the method you prefer. Refer to the photo of the finished

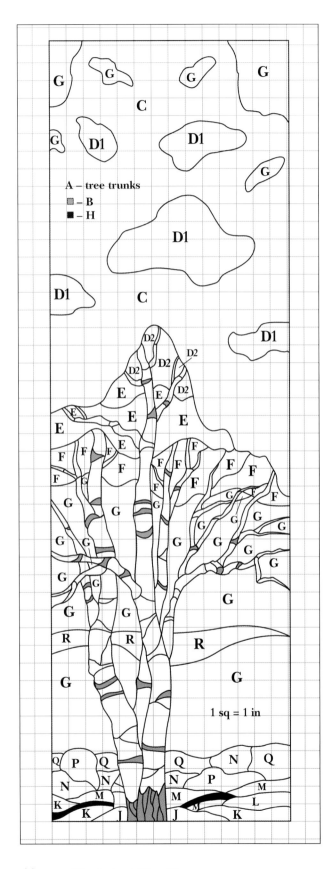

A – tree trunks
□ – B
■ – H

D2

1 sq = 1 in

mosaic as a guide for tesserae placement. Instructions specific to this project are as follows:

1 Cut (pp16–23) and shape (pp24–26) all required tesserae as indicated on pattern.

• When tracing the pattern lines of the tree trunks and branches (A) and the sky areas (G, R), arrange these pieces on the glass sheets with the grain (streaks and flow of color) running horizontally. By positioning the pieces in this manner, the birch trees will appear more realistic and the sky will have wisps of cloud scattered throughout.

2 Lay glass shapes that depict trees (A, B), sky (G,R), groundcover, and distant foliage (J – Q), first. Leave area to be filled with small polished stones (H) empty, to be filled at a later stage.

3 Apply the foliage (C, D1) in the forefront, randomly placing the various sizes of square tesserae throughout the outlined areas without forming a structured grid. The underside of the tesserae (C) is covered with thin pieces of green and brown glass referred to as fractures. This colorful handmade art glass is often used in stained glass panels to represent foliage. Add depth and interest to the mosaic by turning over the tesserae so that the fracture-covered side will be exposed on the front surface of the mosaic.

4 Fill in the remaining foliage (D2, E, F) with random-sized tesserae, shaping a tessera as necessary to fill in any small space.

5 When all mosaic pieces have been applied to the vinyl, follow the instructions for Applying Mosaic to the Base/Support Structure (p35).

6 Carefully run a utility knife (with a fresh blade) through the vinyl and around the perimeter of the empty areas of the riverbed. Slowly peel away the vinyl without dislodging any surrounding glass pieces from the adhesive. Press small polished stones (H) into the exposed adhesive to fill the empty area and form the riverbed.

7 Once the adhesive has set, follow the instructions for Applying Grout (pp30–31) and Cleaning the Finished Piece (p31).

Heartbeat
Wall Mirror

MOSAIC PANEL DIMENSIONS
23¹⁄₄ in high x 22¹⁄₂ in wide

MOSAIC MATERIAL REQUIRED
A 14 in x 18 in 3mm mirror
B 12 in x 24 in iridescent translucent red with white wispy art glass
(cut into ³⁄₄ in x ³⁄₄ in tesserae)

Letters refer to type and quantity of mosaic material used for pattern on page 69. The quantities and types listed are the minimum requirements for completing this project as illustrated, but materials may be substituted and quantities modified as necessary.

Specific and/or Additional Materials and Tools Required

MATERIALS

24 in x 24 in piece of
  exterior grade plywood
Black non-sanded grout

TOOLS

Jigsaw

Base/Support Structure

Guidelines for constructing a base are given in Making Wood Base/Support Structures for Mosaics (pp36–37). Specific instructions for this project are as follows:

1 Trace the perimeter of heart outline onto sheet of plywood.
2 Using a jigsaw, cut out the heart shape along the traced outline.
3 Sandpaper edges smooth.
4 Use a pattern copy to trace (pp15–16) the outline of the two pieces of 3mm mirror (A) accurately onto the base. The mirror pieces must be $^7/_8$ in apart to accommodate the placement of a row of $^3/_4$ in square tesserae between them.
5 Key (score) the plywood surface with a utility knife to aid adhesion.

Mosaic Instructions

Construct the mosaic mirror by following instructions given for Direct Method (pp26–31). Refer to the photograph (p68) for tesserae placement. Instructions specific to this project are as follows:

1 Cut (pp16–23) and shape (pp24–26) the 2 pieces of 3mm mirror (A) as indicated on the pattern. Smooth (pp24–26) the mirror pieces with wet/dry sandpaper or a diamond pad to finish the outside edges.
2 Adhere the mirror pieces to the base with a non-corrosive tile adhesive that will not cause harm to the silver backing.
3 To outline and accentuate the shape of a heart, the $^3/_4$ in tesserae (B) are positioned and adhered to the base in the opus vermiculatum (p31) style

of mosaic construction. Beginning at the lower portion of the heart, apply a row of tesserae around the perimeter of the mirror piece on the left side. The interstices (spaces) between tesserae should be approximately $^1/_{16}$ in. Using a glass cutter or mosaic nippers, trim tesserae to fit where the ends of the row meet at the bottom of the heart.
4 Outline the mirror piece on the right side with a row of tesserae, starting at the top left corner of the piece and working downwards. Trim tesserae to fit at the juncture where the end of the row meets the row outlining the left mirror piece.
5 From the top of the base (at the point the two sides meet), lay a row of tesserae

along the outside edge. Tesserae should not protrude past the edge of the base. Trim tesserae at the end of each row as it meets with the rows already in position.

6 When entire perimeter row has been adhered, start a new row within the one just completed. Working inwards towards center, fill in remainder of mosaic in the same manner. Trim each tessera to fit into spaces that are not large enough to accommodate a whole piece.

7 With the base lying flat on work surface, adhere tesserae along outside edge of plywood, approximately $1/16$ in apart.

8 Once adhesive has cured (approximately 24 hours), follow instructions for Applying Grout (pp30–31) and Cleaning Finished Piece (p31).

9 Refer to Mounting Mosaic Wall Pieces (p37) to hang finished mosaic. The irregular shape of the mirror allows it to be hung at any angle.

Tips for working with larger pieces of mirror

• Always cut mirror on glass side, not the silvered underside.

• Small chips may appear in the silvering along the edge of a mirror when grinding or shaping a piece to fit the pattern. These chips can be visible once the mirror is adhered in place and can mar the appearance of the finished mosaic. Chips can be removed or lessened by smoothing the silvered edge at a 45° angle using a glass grinder, wet/dry sandpaper, diamond pad, or carborundum stone, Refer to Smoothing Jagged and Sharp Edges on Mosaic Pieces (pp24–26) for specific instructions about tools and techniques.

• To prevent damage or discoloration to the silver backing, always use non-corrosive tile adhesives, mirror mastic, or neutral curing silicone.

• Sanded grout is gritty and may scratch mirrored surfaces even after it has cured. Use a smooth, non-sanded grout whenever possible or use a grout sealer on sanded versions to keep the sand particles affixed between the interstices.

• Cover the mirror surface with a single layer of overlapping rows of masking tape to prevent scratches while applying tesserae and/or sanded grout.

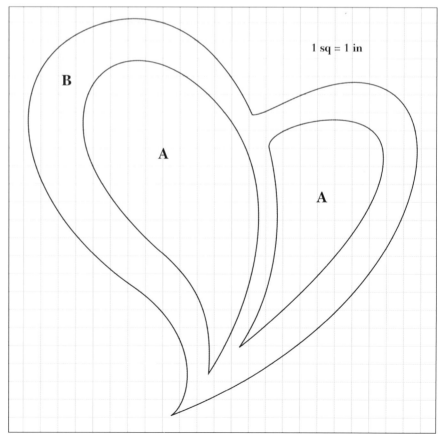

1 sq = 1 in

B

A

A

Inukshuk Panorama
Wall Hanging

MOSAIC PANEL DIMENSIONS
$9^{1}/_{2}$ in high x $43^{1}/_{2}$ in wide

MOSAIC MATERIAL REQUIRED

A   13 in x 40 in mirrored dark blue semi-antique art glass
B   6 in x 6 in mirrored dark amber semi-antique art glass
C   6 in x 6 in mirrored turquoise semi-antique art glass
D   6 in x 12 in dark brown and white opal art glass
E   6 in x 12 in charcoal gray and white opal art glass
F   6 in x 12 in wispy white and pale gray art glass
G   14 in x 14 in water-textured soft white art glass
H   6 in x 6 in medium purple semi-translucent art glass
J   12 in x 6 in white with brick red opal art glass
NOTE *The letter I is not used in this listing*
Letters refer to type and quantity of mosaic material used for pattern on page 71. The
quantities and types listed are the minimum requirements for completing this project as
illustrated, but materials may be substituted and quantities modified as necessary.

Specific and/or Additional Materials and Tools Required

MATERIALS
Heavy-duty masking tape
Glass etching cream (optional)
Black sanded grout

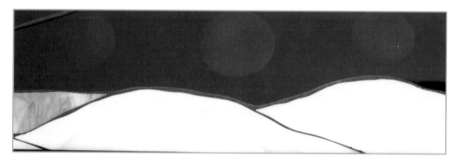

Basic/Support Structure

• 1 piece 9½ in x 43½ in x ¾ in exterior grade plywood with wood trim moldings around the outside edge. Guidelines for constructing a base with wood trim moldings are given in Making Wood Base/Support Structures for Mosaics (pp36–37).

Mosaic Instructions

Construct mosaic panel by following instructions given for Direct Method (pp26–31). Refer to photo of finished mosaics as a guide for tesserae placement. Instructions specific to this project are as follows:

1 Cut (pp16–23) and shape (pp24–26) all required tesserae. See pattern on this page.

2 Surfaces of three sky pieces (A) have been lightly etched with circular shapes to illustrate the nightly passage of the moon. To do this refer to photos on p49 and follow these steps:

• Cover the top surface of glass pieces with heavy-duty masking tape.

• Trace moon shapes on the masking tape (see pattern).

• Use utility knife (with a fresh blade) to cut masking tape along traced lines, not pressing too hard and scoring glass surface below. Remove cut masking tape circles, revealing glass surface below. The exposed surface can be lightly sandblasted to create the full moon effect. If you do not have sandblasting equipment use glass etching cream available at craft and/or hardware stores. Follow the manufacturer's instructions and apply etching cream to exposed glass surfaces. Carefully wash cream away, unveiling moon shapes below.

3 Opus sectile (p31) is used for this project. Individual pieces are cut, shaped, and laid out like a stained glass window. Adhere largest pieces to the base/support structure first and then complete mosaic design by attaching remaining smaller tesserae. Put the mosaic aside. Allow adhesive to set 24 hours.

4 Follow instructions for Applying Grout (pp30–31) and Cleaning Finished Piece (p31).

5 Refer to Mounting Mosaic Wall Pieces (pp36–37) for instructions on hanging finished mosaic.

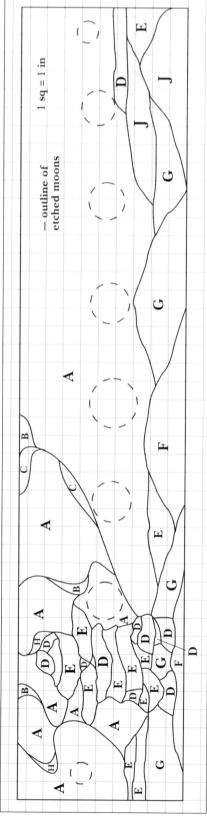

-- outline of etched moons

1 sq = 1 in

A Safe Place
Curio Cabinet

MOSAIC PANEL DIMENSIONS

2 roof panels 7 3/4 in high x 5 1/2 in wide

2 side panels 12 in high x 5 1/2 in wide

2 door panels 10 in high x 4 in wide

MOSAIC MATERIAL REQUIRED

A   16 in x 10 in white, brown, and gray opal art glass

B   16 in x 20 in blue, gray, and white ring mottle art glass (cut into random-size tesserae)

C   18 – 3/4 in x 3/4 in translucent green and copper vitreous glass mosaic tiles

D   18 – 3/4 in x 3/4 in translucent brown and copper vitreous glass mosaic tiles

E   6 in x 6 in emerald, spring, and light green ring mottle art glass

F   6 in x 6 in blue, emerald green, and white ring mottle art glass

Letters refer to type and quantity of mosaic material used for patterns on page 74. The quantities and types listed are the minimum requirements for completing this project as illustrated, but materials may be substituted and quantities modified as necessary.

Specific and/or Additional Materials and Tools Required

MATERIALS
Wood curio cabinet (over all measures 20 in high x 13 1/2 in wide x 7 in deep)
Charcoal sanded grout

Base/Support Structure
A pre-made wood curio cabinet is the base/support structure for this mosaic project. Adjust the patterns as necessary to fit the dimensions and configurations of the cabinet chosen for your project.

Mosaic Instructions
To expedite the mosaic process, construct panels using Indirect (Reverse) Method (pp32–35). By assembling the panels on separate sheets of clear adhesive-backed vinyl, less time and effort will be spent gluing mosaic to base/support structure. However, Direct Method (pp26–31) can be used if it is the method you prefer.

Grout seam where side panel and roof panel adjoin.

Refer to photo of finished mosaic as a guide for tesserae placement. Instructions specific to this project are as follows:

1 Cut (pp16–23) and shape (pp24–26) all required tesserae on the patterns.

• When tracing pattern lines of tree trunks and branches, arrange the pieces on glass sheet (A) with grain (streaks and flow of color) running horizontally. By positioning the pieces in this manner, the glass will resemble birch bark more closely and the trees will have a more natural appearance.

• Cut the glass mosaic tiles (C, D) into random triangular shapes that resemble leaves.

2 Lay glass shapes representing tree trunks and limbs (A) and ground areas (E, F) first. Shaded pattern areas on the trees and in background are left free of tesserae. These areas are design elements that will be visible once the spaces are filled with grout.

3 Intersperse the leaf-like shapes (C, D) throughout the branches and below, giving the appearance of foliage on the trees as well as leaves falling to the ground.

4 Fill in remaining background sky (B) with random-size tesserae, shaping a tessera as necessary to fill in any small space.

5 Once all mosaic panels have been adhered to the base/support structure, set the cabinet aside until the adhesive has cured for approximately 24 hours.

6 Follow instructions for Applying Grout (pp30–31) and Cleaning Finished Piece (p31).

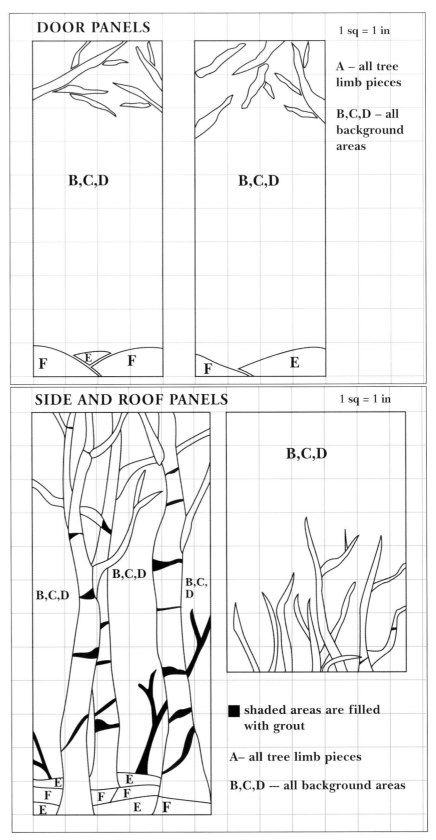

DOOR PANELS

1 sq = 1 in

A – all tree limb pieces

B,C,D – all background areas

B,C,D

B,C,D

F E F

F E

SIDE AND ROOF PANELS

1 sq = 1 in

B,C,D

B,C,D

B,C,D

B,C,D

B,C, D

E E
F F/F
E E F

■ shaded areas are filled with grout

A– all tree limb pieces

B,C,D --- all background areas

A Boy and His Dragon
Shield Mirror

MOSAIC PANEL DIMENSIONS
22$\frac{1}{2}$ in diameter circle

MOSAIC MATERIAL REQUIRED
A 20 in x 20 in 3mm mirror
B 14 in x 14 in mirrored copper semi-antique art glass
C 6 in x 6 in mirrored turquoise semi-antique art glass
D 6 in x 6 in mirrored dark blue semi-antique art glass
E 6 in x 6 in mirrored light purple semi-antique art glass
F Four 35mm translucent orange faceted glass jewels
G One 40mm large iridescent dark blue glass moon face
Letters refer to type and quantity of mosaic material used for pattern on page 77. The quantities and types listed are the minimum requirements for completing this project as illustrated, but materials may be substituted and quantities modified as necessary.

Specific and/or Additional Materials and Tools Required

MATERIALS
23 in x 23 in piece of $^3/_4$ in exterior grade plywood
4 in x 4 in piece of adhesive-backed reflective foil
Black non-sanded grout

TOOLS
Jigsaw

Base/Support Structure
Guidelines for constructing a base are given in Making Wood Base/Support Structures for Mosaics (pp36–37). Specific instructions for this project are as follows:
1 Trace the perimeter of 22 in diameter circle onto plywood.

2 Using a jigsaw, cut out circle along traced outline.
3 Sand edges smooth.
4 Use a pattern copy to trace the pattern accurately onto the base.
5 Key (score) plywood surface with utility knife to aid adhesion.

Mosaic Instructions
Construct mosaic mirror by following instructions given for the Direct Method (pp26–31). Refer to the photograph of finished mosaic for tesserae placement. Instructions specific to this project are as follows:
1 Cut and shape (pp16–23) 4 pieces of the 3mm mirror (A) as on the pattern. Smooth (p67) the mirror pieces with wet/dry sandpaper or a

diamond pad. Refer to Tips for Working with Larger Pieces of Mirror (p69).
2 Adhere (p69) 3mm mirror pieces to base with a non-corrosive tile adhesive.
3 Glue glass moon face (G) and orange faceted glass jewels (F) to base piece. To add sparkle and obscure adhesive beneath glass jewels, cover underside of jewels with an adhesive-backed reflective foil before gluing.
• Wash jewels with soap and water to remove any trace of oil, grease or dirt on surfaces. Buff dry with a lint-free cloth.
• Cut adhesive-backed foil into 4 pieces large enough to cover a single jewel. Peel away waxed paper backing,

position foil over underside of a jewel, and press foil firmly to surface. Burnish foil to the glass, smoothing away any wrinkles.

• Place foiled side of jewels on work surface. Use utility knife (with a fresh blade) to cut along outside edge and remove excess foil. Refer to photo on p55 that illustrates this process.

4 Cut mirrored semi-antique art glasses into specified tesserae:

• copper (B) – cut a 9 in x 9 in piece into $^7/_8$ in x $^7/_8$ in square tesserae; cut a 6 in x 6 in piece into $^3/_4$ in high x 1$^1/_2$ in wide triangles; cut remainder into random-size rectangular tesserae

• turquoise (C) – cut into $^3/_4$ in high x 1$^1/_2$ in wide triangles.

• dark blue (D) and light purple (E) – cut into random-size rectangular tesserae

5 Adhere triangular (B, C) and random-size rectangular (B, D, E) tesserae to base/ support structure as shown in photo of finished mosaic.

6 Lay base flat on work surface, and adhere square tesserae (B) along outside plywood edge, $^1/_{16}$ in apart. Allow 24 hours for adhesive to set.

7 Use a diamond pad or wet/dry sandpaper to lightly sand away rough areas along top edge of tesserae attached around the shield perimeter.

8 Follow the instructions for Applying Grout (pp30–31) and Cleaning Finished Piece (p31).

9 Refer to Mounting Mosaic Wall Pieces (p37) for instructions on hanging the finished mosaic.

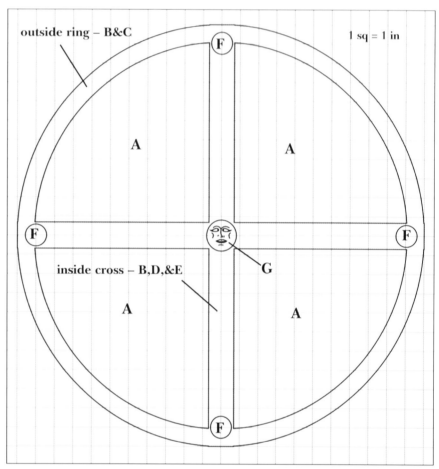

A Boy and His Dragon
Sword Clothes Rack

MOSAIC PANEL DIMENSIONS

32$\frac{1}{2}$ in high x 10$\frac{1}{2}$ in wide

MOSAIC MATERIAL REQUIRED

A 6 in x 22 in 3mm mirror

B 12 in x 20 in mirrored copper semi-antique art glass

C 12 in x 14 in mirrored turquoise semi-antique art glass

D 6 in x 6 in mirrored dark blue semi-antique art glass

E One 35mm translucent orange faceted glass jewel

F Two 30mm medium iridescent dark blue glass moon faces

Letters refer to type and quantity of mosaic material used for pattern on page 79. The quantities and types listed are the minimum requirements for completing this project as illustrated, but materials may be substituted and quantities modified as necessary.

Specific and/or Additional Materials and Tools Required

MATERIALS
20 in x 34 in piece of $\frac{3}{4}$ in exterior grade plywood
Wood trim moldings
Five #8 wood screws (1 in long)
2 coat hooks and screws
Black non-sanded grout
Two 2 in Z-clip low-profile fasteners

TOOLS
Jigsaw
Power drill

Base/Support Structure
Guidelines for constructing a base are given in Making Wood Base/Support Structures for Mosaics (pp36–37). Specific instructions for this project are as follows:

1 Trace the outline of the main base piece and the sword onto the sheet of plywood.
2 Cut main base piece from the larger sheet of plywood. Attach the wood moldings to the 5 sides around the perimeter of the base.
3 Using a jigsaw, cut out the sword shape along the traced outlines.
4 Sandpaper edges smooth .
5 Use a pattern copy to trace the pattern lines accurately onto the main base piece and the sword.
6 Attach the sword shape to the base/support structure as indicated by the pattern. Spread a thin layer of carpenter's glue on the underside of sword and apply it to base piece. Use a power drill to fasten sword securely to the base with wood screws, countersink screws until they are flush with plywood surface.
7 Fasten coat hooks to main base in the desired location.
8 Key (score) plywood surface with a utility knife to aid adhesion.

Mosaic Instructions
Construct clothes rack by following the instructions given for the Direct Method (pp26–31). Refer to the photo of the finished mosaic as a guide for tesserae placement. Instructions specific to this project are as follows:

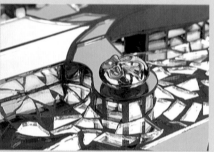

1 Cut and shape (pp16–26) mirrored glass pieces of a specific shape before cutting the tesserae.

• 3mm mirror (A) – cut pieces for front of sword; measure and cut $^3/_4$ in wide pieces for side of blade; cut ten – $^3/_4$ in x $^1/_2$ in tesserae to go on side of handle tip; cut remainder into random-size tesserae for the background.

• copper (B) – cut 2 pieces for front of sword grip; cut twenty $^3/_4$ in x $^1/_2$ in tesserae for side of handle grip; cut thirty 1 in high x 2 in wide triangles for border; cut remainder into random-size tesserae for background.

• turquoise (C) – cut 4 pieces for front of sword guard; cut 26 triangles for border 1 in high x 2 in wide and the 2 pieces located at the bottom tip of the base and the piece in the middle of the top row of the border; cut remainder into $^3/_4$ in x $^3/_8$ in tesserae for the side of the sword guard.

• dark blue (D) – cut into random-size tesserae for background.

2 Smooth (p67) mirror pieces for front of sword with wet/dry sandpaper or a diamond pad to attain a tidy, finished look along outside edges. Refer to Tips for Working with Larger Pieces of Mirror (p69).

3 Adhere (p69) mirrored pieces to base with a non-corrosive tile adhesive. Apply the various pieces to front and sides of the sword before the border and background are filled in. Cut any triangular tesserae to fit as necessary. Refer to photo of finished mosaic for placement and color disbursement of random-size background tesserae.

4 Glue orange faceted glass jewel (E) and glass moon faces (F) to mirrored surfaces of sword using clear silicone or any clear adhesive for glass surfaces. Set project aside for 24 hours while adhesive sets.

5 Follow instructions for Applying Grout (pp30–31) and Cleaning Finished Piece (p31).

6 Refer to Mounting Mosaic Wall Pieces (p37) for instructions on hanging finished mosaic. Use two 2 in Z-clip low-profile fasteners to mount clothes rack flush against wall and to evenly distribute its weight. If possible, anchor clothes rack to studs located in the wall.

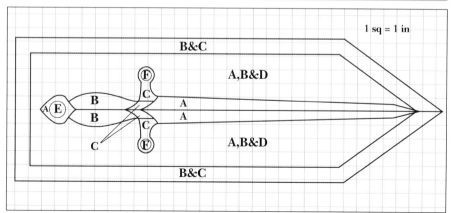

1 sq = 1 in

A Boy and His Dragon
Bookcase / Cupboard

Specific and/or Additional Materials and Tools Required

MATERIALS
4 ft x 8 ft sheet of $^{1}/_{2}$ in exterior grade plywood

Two 32-in-long piano hinges and screws

7$^{1}/_{2}$ ft wood cap molding

4$^{1}/_{2}$ ft wood trim molding

Black non-sanded grout

TOOLS
Jigsaw

Power drill

Base/Support Structure
Guidelines for constructing a base and a list of tools and materials are given in Making Wood Base/Support Structures for Mosaics (pp36–37). Refer to the accompanying photos for assistance in putting cabinet together. Specific instructions for this project are as follows:

1 Trace outline of back, sides, and wing-shaped doors onto plywood.

2 Cut the pieces from the larger sheet of plywood. Use a jigsaw to cut the curved lines.

3 Cut 3 shelves from remaining plywood; 14 in x 10$^{1}/_{2}$ in; 16$^{1}/_{2}$ in x 10$^{1}/_{2}$ in; 19 in x 10$^{1}/_{2}$ in

4 Cut a right angled notch along the length of the back inside edge of the side panels.

5 Sandpaper all edges smooth.

6 Apply a bead of carpenter's glue along notch on both side panels and fit back panel into

notches. Fasten panels to back piece with finishing nails.

7 Mark position of shelves on both sides of side panels. Fasten 1 shelf at a time to side panels and back panel. Apply a bead of glue to back and both outside edges of a shelf and slide it into marked position and nail in place. Fasten wood trim molding to front of each shelf to finish exposed edge.

8 Measure and cut lengths of wood cap molding for the seams between side and back panels and bottom edges of the side panels. Apply glue to the grooves of the cap molding and nail them in place.

9 Attach the wing doors to the front edge of side panels using 2 piano hinges.

10 Cover all nail holes with wood filler and sand smooth.

11 Use a pattern copy to trace pattern lines accurately onto the 3 panels and wing doors.

12 Key (score) plywood surfaces with a utility knife to aid adhesion.

Mosaic Instructions

Follow Direct Method instructions (pp26–31) to apply mosaic materials to side panels, dragon head, and wing panels. Refer to photos of finished panels for tesserae placement.

1 Cut and shape (pp16–24) glass shapes as on pattern. Smooth (p67) mirror pieces with wet/dry sandpaper or a diamond pad to attain a tidy edge that aligns with outside edge of bookcase/cupboard. Refer to Tips for Working with Larger Pieces of Mirror (p69).

2 Adhere (p67) mirrored glass pieces to base with a non-corrosive tile adhesive.

3 Glue remaining glass pieces and nuggets to cupboard. Cut several glass nuggets in half and glue (cut side to base) to form ridges over brow, around nostril, and along dragon's smile. Set bookcase aside for 24 hours to set.

4 Follow instructions for Applying Grout (pp30–31) and Cleaning Finished Piece (p31).

5 Paint or stain any exposed wood edge or cover with tesserae to finish the unit.

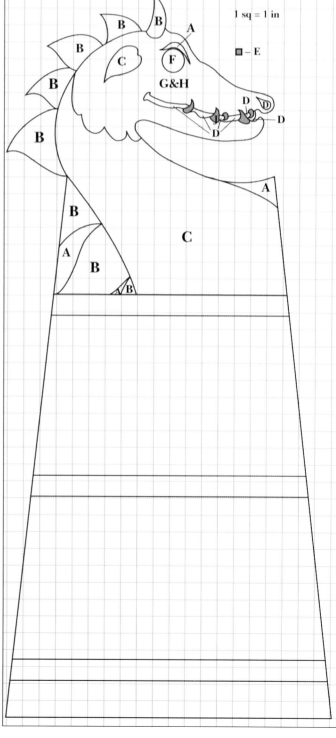

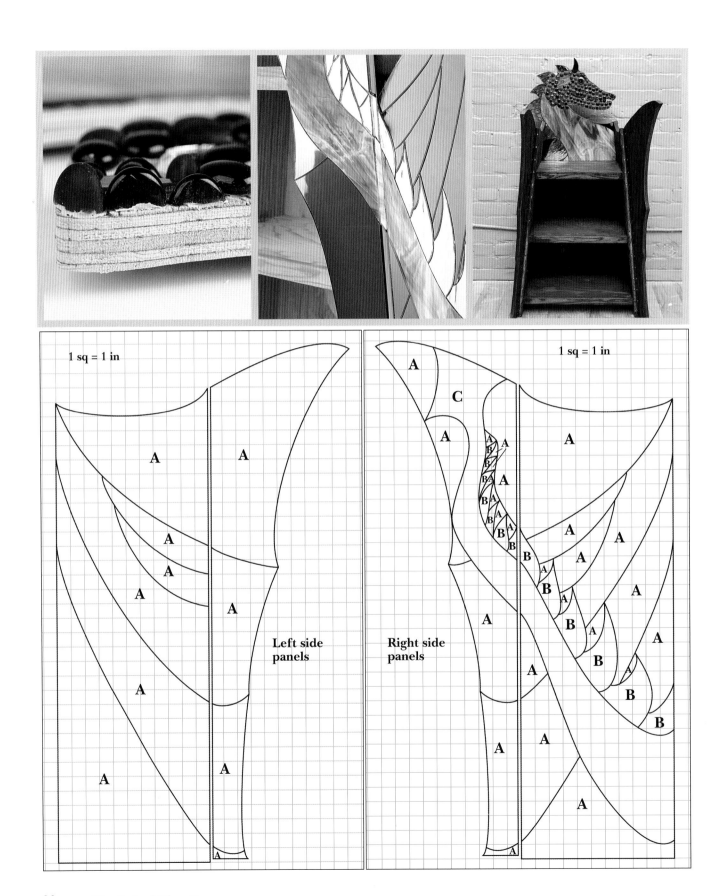

1 sq = 1 in

1 sq = 1 in

A

C

A

A

A

A

A

A

A

B

B

B

A

B

A

A

B

A

A

A

B

A

A

A

A

A

A

A

A

B

A

A

A

A

A

B

A

B

B

B

A

A

A

A

A

A

A

A

A

A

A

A

A

A

A

A

Left side panels

Right side panels

Rose Nouveau
Tabletop

Specific and/or Additional Materials and Tools Required

MATERIALS

Ivory sanded grout
13$\frac{1}{2}$ in x 15$\frac{1}{2}$ in $\frac{3}{4}$ in exterior grade plywood
Grout sealant
13$\frac{1}{2}$ in x 15$\frac{1}{2}$ in sheet of 6mm clear glass (optional)
4 acrylic bumper pads (optional)

Basic/Support Structure

• 1 piece of 13$\frac{1}{2}$ x 15$\frac{1}{2}$ in exterior grade $\frac{3}{4}$ in plywood. Guidelines for constructing a wood base are given in Making Wood Base/Support Structures for Mosaics (pp36–37).

Mosaic Instructions

Make mosaic tabletop using either the Direct Method (pp26–31) or Indirect (Reverse) Method (pp32–35). Refer to photo of finished mosaic as a guide for tesserae placement. Instructions specific to this project are as follows:

1 Cut, shape (pp16–23), and smooth all edges (pp24–26) of tesserae as indicated on pattern.

2 Adhere glass pieces to base/support structure. Allow to set for 24 hours.

3 The leaf, rose, and stem shapes are a dark contrast to the lighter grout. These interstices between the tesserae are wider than most mosaics and when grout filled accentuate the nouveau rose design. Refer to instructions for Applying Grout (pp30–31) and incorporate these additional steps in the process.

• The mosaic panel (tabletop illustrated) is set into frame of table so did not require a border of wood moldings or tesserae. Use water-dampened sponge to slightly round grout along mosaic perimeter to finish edge.

• Mosaic may require grouting more than once for an even finish. Use sanded grout and slow curing time by placing a small sheet of plastic over the mosaic and occasionally misting with water so grout will dry slower to decrease risk of cracking. If small fissures do appear, apply another thin layer of grout over affected area.

4 When grout cures, refer to Cleaning the Finished Piece (p31).

5 Apply a grout sealant (p30) on tabletop surface or cover with sheet of clear glass if the table is to be used. Attach acrylic bumper pads to underside corners of the glass sheet to help keep it in place.

Wright Style
Headboard

MOSAIC PANEL DIMENSIONS
20 in high x 39 in wide

MOSAIC MATERIAL REQUIRED

A 18 in x 18 in translucent dark blue and white wispy art glass

B 14 in x 14 in opaque light blue and white wispy art glass

C 12 in x 6 in mirrored turquoise semi-antique art glass

D 6 in x 6 in mirrored dark amber semi-antique art glass

E 9 in x 4 in opaque iridescent amber art glass

F 12 in x 12 in granite-textured iridescent blues, yellow, and gold-pink streaky art glass

G 12 in x 12 in opaque pale lavender and white wispy art glass

H 12 in x 12 in opaque light amber and white wispy art glass

J 16 in x 16 in opaque iridescent pale amber and white wispy art glass

K 4 in x 8 in turquoise and brown with mini fractures art glass

L 12 in x 12 in catspaw-textured opaque amber art glass

M 12 in x 6 in white and pale amber wispy art glass

N 12 in x 12 in opaque iridescent pale lavender and white wispy art glass

NOTE *The letter I is not used in this listing*

Letters refer to type and quantity of mosaic material used for pattern on p 89. The quantities and types listed are the minimum requirements for completing this project as illustrated, but materials may be substituted and quantities modified as necessary

---

Specific and/or Additional Materials and Tools Required

MATERIALS
Dark blue sanded grout
Three – 2 in Z-clip low-profile
  fasteners

TOOLS
Screwdriver or power drill

Base/Support Structure
• 1 piece 21 in x 39 in of ³/₄ in exterior grade plywood cut into the headboard shape (see pattern) with wood trim moldings around outside edge. Guidelines are given in Making Wood Base/Support Structures for Mosaics (pp36–37).

Mosaic Instructions
Construct mosaic headboard panel by following the instructions given for the Direct Method (pp26–31). Refer to the photograph of the finished mosaic as a guide for tesserae placement. Specific instructions follows:
1 Cut and shape (pp16–26) tesserae as indicated on the pattern p89).

• Pieces cut from art glass selections F and K are adhered to the base/support structure with textured underside turned upwards. Turn pattern over and trace reverse image of pattern shapes onto the smooth top surface of glass sheet to be cut.

2 Use opus sectile (p31) tesserae style for this project. Individual pieces are cut, shaped, and laid out like a stained glass window. Adhere largest pieces to base first and then complete mosaic design with remaining smaller tesserae. Allow adhesive to set 24 hours.

3 Follow the instructions for Applying Grout (pp30–31) and Cleaning Finished Piece (p31).

4 Refer to Mounting Mosaic Wall Pieces (p37) for general instructions on hanging the finished mosaic. Use three 2 in Z-clip low-profile fasteners to mount the headboard flush against the wall and evenly distribute its weight. If possible, anchor the headboard to studs located in the wall. Refer to the photograph for hardware placement on the back of headboard.

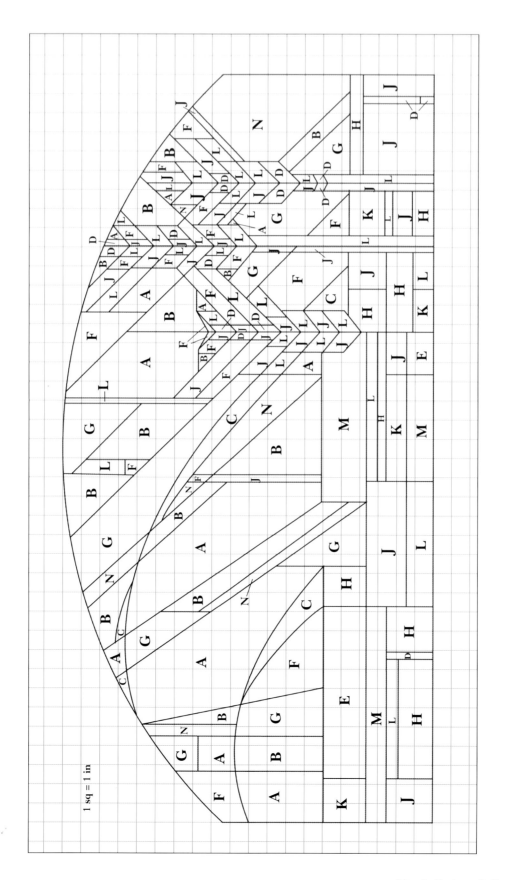

1 sq = 1 in

Wright Style
Nightstand

MOSAIC PANEL DIMENSIONS

2 side panels 5$\frac{1}{8}$ in high x 7 in wide
1 top panel 7 in high x 12 in wide

MOSAIC MATERIAL REQUIRED

A   12 in x 12 in translucent dark blue and white wispy art glass
B   6 in x 12 in opaque light blue and white wispy art glass
C   8 in x 8 in opaque pale lavender and white wispy art glass
D   9 in x 2 in mirrored turquoise semi-antique art glass
E   2 in x 2 in mirrored dark amber semi-antique art glass
F   2 in x 2 in granite-textured iridescent blues, yellow, and gold-pink streaky art glass
G   2 in x 2 in catspaw-textured opaque amber art glass
H   4 in x 8 in opaque iridescent pale lavender and white wispy art glass

Letters refer to type and quantity of mosaic material used for pattern on page 91. The quantities and types listed are the minimum requirements for completing this project as illustrated, but materials may be substituted and quantities modified as necessary.

Specific and/or Additional Materials and Tools Required

MATERIALS
20 in x 28 in piece of $\frac{3}{4}$ in exterior grade plywood
Dark blue sanded grout
Two – 2 in Z-clip low-profile fasteners

TOOLS
Screwdriver or power drill

Base/Support Structure
Some general guidelines and the materials and tools required for constructing a base with wood trim molding are given in Making Wood Base/Support Structures for Mosaics (pp36–37). If you do not have the necessary skills and tools for basic woodworking ask a friend or colleague that does to make this simple nightstand base. To construct the nightstand base/support structure:
1 Cut 5 pieces of $\frac{3}{4}$ in exterior grade plywood: 2 pieces (top and bottom) – 11 in x 7$\frac{1}{2}$ in; 2 pieces (sides) – 5$\frac{1}{8}$ in x 7$\frac{1}{2}$ in; 1 piece (back) – 5$\frac{3}{8}$ in x 12$\frac{1}{4}$ in.
2 Glue and nail top and bottom pieces between two side pieces to form a cube. Back piece is then glued and nailed over opening at one end of cube.
3 Cut lengths of wood cap molding to frame the edges of the back and front opening of nightstand. The ends of each piece of molding must be cut at a 45° angle to achieve a fitted, finished looking corner. Glue and nail moldings in place.
4 Fill nail holes with wood filler, smooth with sandpaper.
5 Choose a stain or paint that complements the color of grout or the mosaic glass selection to finish the wood trim as well as the back and underside of the nightstand.

Mosaic Instructions

Construct mosaic for top and side panels by following instructions given for Direct Method (p26–31). Refer to photograph of finished mosaic as a guide for tesserae placement. Instructions specific to this project are as follows:

1 Cut and shape (pp16–26) all required tesserae as indicated on the pattern on this page.

• The piece cut from art glass selection F is adhered to base/support structure with textured underside turned upwards. Turn pattern over and trace reverse image of pattern shape onto smooth top surface of glass sheet to be cut.

2 Opus sectile (p31) is the tesserae style used for this project. Individual pieces are cut, shaped, and laid out in a manner reminiscent of a stained glass window. Adhere pieces to the sides of nightstand before assembling top mosaic surface. Once tesserae have been glued to the three surfaces put nightstand aside for approximately 24 hours to allow adhesive to set.

3 Follow instructions for Applying Grout (pp30–31) and Cleaning Finished Piece (p31).

4 Refer to Mounting Mosaic Wall Pieces (p37) for general instructions on hanging the finished mosaic. Use two – 2 in Z-clip low-profile fasteners to secure nightstand flush against the wall and to evenly distribute its weight. If possible, anchor nightstand to studs located in the wall.

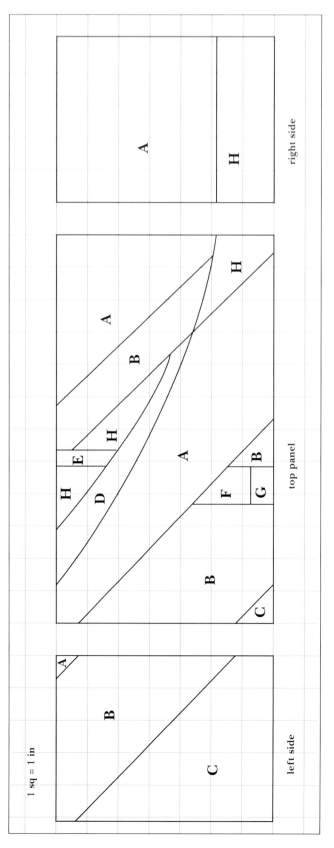

Phoenix Rising
Garden Marker

MOSAIC PANEL DIMENSIONS

4 panels – 20 in high by 8 in wide at base x 2 in wide at top

MOSAIC MATERIAL REQUIRED

A   3 in x 6 in yellow and white wispy art glass

B   16 in x 18 in orange red and white wispy art glass

C   18 in x 24 in charcoal gray and white opal art glass (cut into random-size tesserae)

Letters refer to type and quantity of art glass used for patterns on page 94. The quantities and types listed are the minimum requirements for completing this project as illustrated, but materials may be substituted and quantities modified as necessary.

Specific and/or Additional Materials and Tools Required

MATERIALS

4-side pre-cast cement plinth (20 in high x 8 in wide at base x 2 in wide at top)

Thin-set mortar

Liquid latex polymer additive (optional)

Basic/Support Structure

Pre-cast cement plinths can be purchased in a variety of styles and are available at home and garden centers. Make a form to cast your own plinth from ³/₄ in exterior grade plywood. Once cement has been poured into the form and cured, the mosaic can be applied to the exterior of the plinth. Adjust patterns as necessary to fit the dimensions and configurations of the plinth chosen for your project.

Mosaic Instructions

Construct the panels using the Indirect (Reverse) Method (pp32–35). By assembling the panels on separate sheets of clear adhesive-backed vinyl, less time and effort will be spent cementing the mosaics to the base/support structure. If preferred, use the Direct Method (pp26–31). Refer to the photograph of the finished garden marker as a guide for tesserae placement. Instructions specific to this project are as follows:

1 The garden marker illustrated has 4 sides covered with mosaic panels of alternating designs. Cut and shape (pp16–24) all tesserae, as indicated on patterns (p94), to complete 2 panels of each design.

2 Lay glass shapes representing the sun (A), phoenix (B), and flames (B) onto the clear adhesive-backed vinyl first.

3 Fill in background with random-size tesserae (C), shaping a tessera as necessary to fill in any small space.

4 Prepare enough mortar to cover the exterior of the plinth. Add dry mortar mix to water and mix to a thick, smooth, creamy consistency. Allow mixture to slake for 10 minutes. For exact measurements of water, dry mortar mix, etc., read and follow manufacturer's directions. For added bond

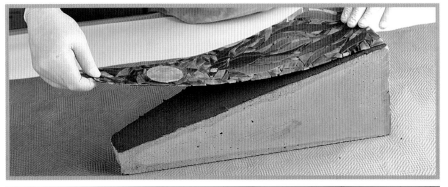

strength and water resistance, use a liquid latex polymer additive in place of water.

5 Use a trowel to spread a layer of mortar mix (approximately $^1/_{16}$ in to $^1/_8$ in thick) over the surface of one side. Adhere a mosaic panel to the plinth by following the instructions for Applying Mosaic to the Base/Support Structure (p35). Also refer to photographs of procedure on p34.

6 Repeat step 5 to adhere remaining mosaic panels to the plinth, alternating the design of panels from one side to the next.

7 Once the four mosaic panels are adhered to base/support structure, set the plinth aside until the mortar has cured for approximately 24 hours.

8 Remove the vinyl, exposing top surface of mosaic panels.

9 Using thin-set mortar mix, follow the instructions for Applying Grout (pp30–31) to fill the interstices between mosaic pieces. Grout seam between each adjacent panel, creating a smooth transition from one side of the plinth to another.

10 Let the mortar set for 24 hours before following the steps for Cleaning the Finished Piece (p31).

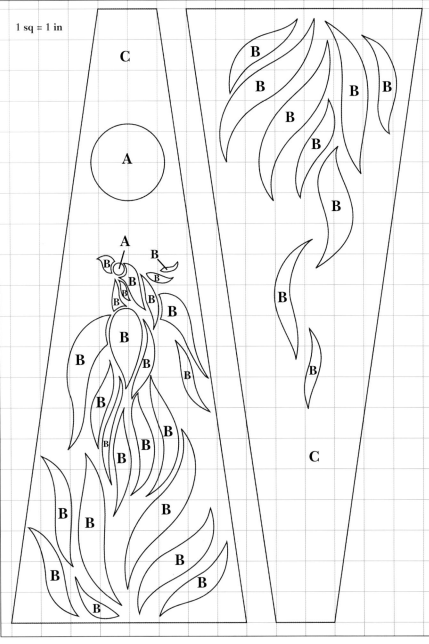

1 sq = 1 in

Translucent Mosaics

The Basic Steps

Translucent mosaics are an interesting variation of the traditional styles and opaque materials that rely on reflective surface properties for visual impact. Constructed by bonding translucent tesserae to a semitransparent base/support structure, light illuminates colors and textures of the mosaic from within.

Listed below are basic materials and tools required to construct translucent mosaic projects. Additional listings with specific requirements are provided for each project. Please review Safety Practices and Equipment (p13) before starting a project.

MATERIALS
- 2 copies of pattern
- Translucent base/support structure for mosaic
- Mosaic materials for project - art glass, glass nuggets and jewels, found objects, etc.
- Newspaper
- Dish soap and water
- Masking tape
- Clear silicone adhesive
- Small disposable container
- Isopropyl (rubbing) alcohol
- Tile grout
- Water

TOOLS
- Apron & safety glasses
- Utility knife or scissors
- Permanent water-proof fine-tipped marker
- Cork-backed straightedge
- Glass cutter & tile and/or glass mosaic nippers
- Running & breaking/grozing pliers
- Small containers or jars
- Smoothing device – carborundum stone, wet/dry sandpaper, diamond pad, or glass grinder
- Caulking gun and/or syringe
- Small palette knife or craft stick
- Tweezers and/or dental pick
- Razor blade and/or paint scraper
- Small container for mixing grout
- Respirator or dust mask
- Rubber or latex gloves
- Sponge & soft lint-free cloth
- Soft bristle brushes and/or toothbrush

Preparing the Pattern
1 Make 2 copies (pp14–15) of the pattern.
2 Verify that outline of pattern fits within area to be covered on base/support structure. Adjust pattern copies if any alterations are made to the original pattern.
3 Use one copy as a guide for cutting, breaking, and shaping mosaic pieces to correct size and shape. When cutting materials through which pattern lines are not clearly visible, cut a template (p16) for required pieces from second pattern copy, cutting inside pattern lines.

Preparing the Base/Support Structure
Translucent mosaics allow light to pass through and illuminate individual tesserae rather than light reflecting off the surface. Silicone is a powerful adhesive that becomes transparent once it cures and is suited to adhering glass tesserae to smooth non-porous surfaces. Select a translucent art glass with an interesting texture for base/support structure whenever possible. Textured glass will help disguise an adhesive while still allowing light to pass through it.
1 Smooth (pp24–26) rough edges or surfaces with the appropriate tools or materials.
2 Clean surface of base/support structure with dish soap and water to remove traces of dust, oil, wax, or grease. Glass and other non-porous structures shouldn't require further preparation.

Preparing the Mosaic Pieces and Tesserae
1 For patterns that need a quantity of tesserae of the same shape and size, cut (pp22,23) uniform and/or random tesserae as listed for project. Separate tesserae by size and color and store in small jars or containers until ready for use.

2 Many translucent mosaic projects utilize art glass cut and shaped into distinctive configurations. Use a waterproof marker and a pattern copy as a guide to trace (pp15–16) each piece onto the requisite material.

3 Cut (pp16–22) each traced piece inside the marked pattern lines.

4 Smooth and shape pieces to fit within the pattern lines and/or to dull sharp and jagged edges if necessary (pp24–26). Interstices between tesserae and individual mosaic pieces should be $^1/_{16}$ in to $^1/_8$ in wide to allow for application of grout unless stated otherwise.

5 Clean each piece thoroughly to ensure adhesion to the base. Use soap and water and rinse thoroughly to remove all traces of cutter oil, marker, grinding residue, etc.

Adhering Mosaic Pieces and Tesserae to the Base/Support Structure

The application of tesserae for a translucent mosaic is a variation of the Direct Method (pp26–31) of mosaic construction.

1 Protect areas that will not be covered with adhesive or grout with masking tape.

2 Use masking tape to secure a pattern copy to work surface. Align base piece (textured side facing down) over pattern into correct position.

3 Place tube of silicone into a caulking gun and squeeze a small amount of silicone into a small disposable container. Silicone starts to set or harden once exposed to air, so reseal tube and replenish supply of silicone only as needed.

4 Using a small palette knife, spread a thin layer of adhesive onto the base/support structure in a small area that can be covered with tesserae in approximately 15 minutes. Use just enough silicone to bond tesserae to surface of the base/support structure so silicone does not ooze out from between glass surfaces and around the bottom edges of tesserae. If applied properly, silicone is practically invisible once tesserae are attached to base/support structure. Alternatively,

butter (p27) backs of individual tessera with silicone but this method tends to be messier when silicone is used as an adhesive.

5 To adhere pieces, apply tesserae one section at a time using the pattern beneath base/support structure as your guide. Firmly press a tessera onto base/support structure in the correct position, twisting piece back and forth slightly, to embed it firmly in the silicone. Use a palette knife to remove excess silicone before it sets.

6 If any of the mosaic pieces are not in correct position, pick up the piece that needs adjusting with tweezers, dental picks, or a utility knife. Apply additional silicone, only if required, and reset piece in the mosaic.

7 Set project aside for at least 24 hours (or as recommended by manufacturer) until silicone has cured.

8 After silicone has set, use utility knife or paint scraper to remove any adhesive that is on the surface, taking care not to scratch the tesserae. A cloth moistened with isopropyl (rubbing) alcohol will remove traces of silicone but avoid spilling alcohol directly onto mosaic. Alcohol can compromise the integrity of the silicone bond if it seeps between and under tesserae.

Applying Grout and Cleaning the Finished Mosaic

Follow same instructions for these final stages (pp30–31) as described for Direct Method (p26).

Translucent Mosaic Projects and Patterns

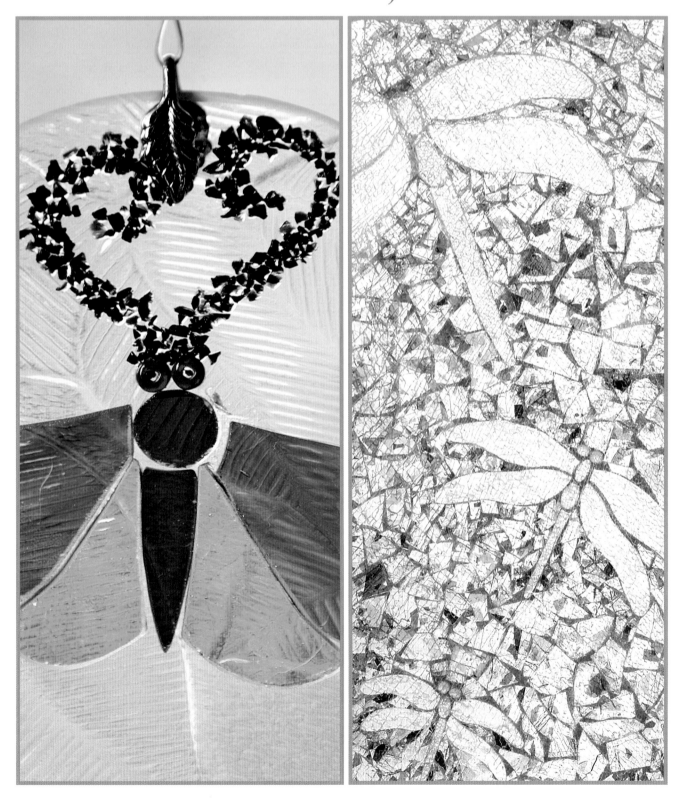

Things with Wings
Bugmobile

MOSAIC DIMENSIONS

5 circular pieces 3³/₈ in diameter

MOSAIC MATERIAL REQUIRED

A 8 in x 11 in leaf textured clear 4mm architectural art glass

B 3 in x 4 in translucent dark gray art glass

C 2 in x 3 in translucent pale green and aqua blue art glass

D 2 in x 2 in translucent teal green art glass

E 1 in x 1 in translucent midnight blue art glass

F 9 translucent red glass beads (7 – 6mm; 2 – 4mm)

G 2 in x 4 in translucent yellow art glass

H 2 in x 3 in translucent orange art glass

J 2 in x 6 in translucent iridescent wispy white art glass

K 1 in x 1 in white and clear wispy art glass

L 2 in x 2 in translucent royal purple art glass

M 2 in x 3 in translucent red art glass

N Six 10mm black glass beads

NOTE *The letter I is not used in this listing*

Letters refer to type and quantity of mosaic material used for patterns on page 101. The quantities and types listed are the minimum requirements for completing this project as illustrated, but materials may be substituted and quantities modified as necessary

Specific and/or Additional Materials and Tools Required

MATERIALS
Black glass frit

5 leaf-shape bails

34 in length of ³/₈ in diameter wood dowel

Carpenter's wood glue

Nylon-coated stainless steel fishing wire (20 lb test)

12 connector sleeves

1 swivel

2 metal spacer beads

Ceiling hook or plant hanger

Paint or stain (optional)

TOOLS
Syringe

Wire cutters

Wood saw (hand or power)

Power drill with ¹/₈ in drill bit

Fine grit sandpaper

Base/Support Structure
Guidelines for making a translucent mosaic base are given in Preparing the Base/Support Structure (p95).

Specific instructions for this project follow:

1 Cut and shape (p19) five 3³/₈ in diameter circles from sheet of textured clear art glass (A).

2 Finish edge on both sides of glass circles. Smooth (pp24–26) away chips or rough areas by sanding edge at 45° with wet/dry sandpaper, diamond pad, or carborundum stone. If a glass grinder is available, hold glass 45° against the diamond bit, rotating circle until entire perimeter has been ground.

3 Fasten a leaf-shaped bail to each glass circle. Dab a small drop of clear silicone (or any clear adhesive used for gluing glass and metal together) on underside of leaf on either side of a bail. Slide the bail over the glass, situating circle between the leaves. Wipe away any oozed adhesive from under the leaves. Place strips of masking tape over leaves until adhesive has cured.

Mosaic Instructions

Apply mosaic pattern to each glass circle following the instructions given for Translucent Mosaics – Basic Steps (pp95–96). See photos p98 to guide tesserae placement. Instructions specific to project are as follows:

1 Cut and shape required tesserae indicated on patterns.
2 Use opus sectile (p31) tesserae style. Individual pieces are cut, shaped, and laid out like a stained glass window. Place a glass circle over a pattern and begin adhering one glass piece at a time to the surface. Butter (p27) entire underside of each piece with a thin layer of silicone and press firmly to base. Use palette knife to remove oozed silicone between glass surfaces. Continue applying tesserae, butting pieces against adjacent ones, as mosaics will not be grouted.

• Fill a small syringe with clear silicone and squeeze slender beads onto base in shape of antennae and/or appendages on pattern. Sprinkle black glass frit over silicone and press frit into silicone using a palette knife or gloved finger. As each base is finished, lift and tilt base and gently tap underside to allow excess frit to fall onto pattern below. Empty frit into a container and use for the next base. Refer to About Glass Frit on p109.

• Eyes are glass beads (F) and glued to the base, see patterns.
• Ladybug – glue black glass beads (N) on top of red wings (M), see the pattern. Fill the shaded area around eyes with black frit.

3 Set project aside for approximately 24 hours until the silicone has cured.

Making the Mobile Apparatus and Hanging the Mosaics

1 Cut one 14 in and one 20 in length of $^3/_8$ in diameter wood dowel with a wood saw.
2 Mark and measure the center and $^1/_4$ in from either side of center point on each dowel. Use chisel or sharp utility knife to cut a $^1/_2$ in wide notch, $^1/_8$ in deep, in center of dowels. Put notched dowels together to form a +, trimming notches for a snug fit. Pull dowels apart, dab a small amount of wood glue in each notch, and fit the dowels back together. Wipe away any glue that has oozed out from the joint and set the apparatus aside until the glue has hardened.
3 Measure and mark the center and $^1/_4$ in from each dowel end. Use a power drill with a $^1/_8$ in bit to drill a hole through each mark. Sand any rough edges and paint or stain the dowels.
4 Use wire cutters to cut one 24 in, two 16 in, two 12 in lengths of nylon-coated steel fishing wire.

5 Thread ends of a 12 in wire through hole of each end of 20 in dowel and 16 in lengths of wire through holes of the 14 in dowel. Thread a connector sleeve onto long end of each wire and slide them up close to dowel. Loop shorter end of the wire over the dowel and back through the sleeve until it protrudes from opposite end $^{1}/_{4}$ in. Pull long end of wires taut until sleeves are $^{1}/_{4}$ in from the dowel.

6 Use wire cutters to gently squeeze the center of the connector sleeves until they are crimped enough that each fishing wire is held firmly in place within a sleeve and cannot be pulled free from either end. Use caution while crimping the sleeves to prevent cutting through the metal or the nylon-coated wire with the cutter blades.

7 Place a second connector sleeve onto the free end of each wire. Thread a wire through the bail loop fastened to a mosaic circle and back through the sleeve. Pull the wire taut until only $^{1}/_{4}$ in extends from the opposite end of the sleeve and the sleeve is $^{1}/_{4}$ in from the bail loop. Crimp the sleeve closed. Fasten 4 mosaic circles in this manner.

8 Thread a connector sleeve and then the swivel onto the 24 in wire length. Loop one wire end back through the sleeve until only $^{1}/_{4}$ in extends from the opposite end. Pull long end of wire taut until sleeve is $^{1}/_{4}$ in from the swivel. Crimp the sleeve closed, securing the swivel in place at one end of the wire length.

9 Thread a connector sleeve onto the free end of the wire and crimp it closed 14 in from the sleeve attached in step 8.

10 Thread the wire end through a metal spacer bead, the center hole of the dowels , the second metal spacer bead, and then through another connector sleeve. Slide the pieces up to the attached sleeve and then crimp the connector sleeve closed to hold them all in place.

11 Slip a connector sleeve onto the free wire end and through bail loop of remaining mosaic circle. Thread wire back through the sleeve until only $^{1}/_{4}$ in extends from opposite end of the sleeve and the sleeve is $^{1}/_{4}$ in from the bail loop. Crimp the sleeve closed.

12 Suspend the bugmobile from a secure ceiling hook near a sunny window or from a plant hook or tree branch in the garden.

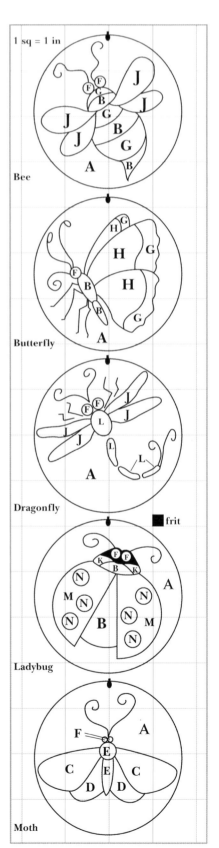

1 sq = 1 in

Bee

Butterfly

Dragonfly

frit

Ladybug

Moth

MOSAIC PANEL DIMENSIONS
11¹/₂ in diameter

MOSAIC MATERIAL REQUIRED

A 1 blue agate/geode slice 2¹/₄ in x 3¹/₂ in

B 30 assorted iridescent translucent blue, white, and clear glass nuggets

C 6 in x 6 in iridescent ice white art glass (cut into ¹/₄ in x ¹/₄ in tesserae)

D 6 in x 6 in lacy white opal art glass (cut into ¹/₄ in x ¹/₄ in tesserae)

E 8 in x 8 in translucent green and blue streaky art glass (cut into small random-size tesserae)

Letters refer to type and quantity of mosaic material used for pattern on page 103. The quantities and types listed are the minimum requirements for completing this project as illustrated, but materials may be substituted and quantities modified as necessary.

Blue-Eyed Daisy
Decorative Plate

Specific and/or Additional Materials and Tools Required

MATERIALS
11½ in diameter clear
  glass plate
Ivory sanded grout

Base/Support Structure
This project is based on an 11½ in diameter clear glass plate. Use any size of glass or ceramic vessel. Adjust pattern and amount of mosaic material required for size of base.

Mosaic Instructions
Follow instructions given for Translucent Mosaics – The Basic Steps (pp95–96). See photo p102 to guide tesserae placement. Instructions specific to this project are as follows:

1 Adjust pattern to accommodate size of plate chosen for project.

2 Place plate upside down over pattern and trace pattern lines onto the underside using a marker.

3 Butter entire underside of agate/geode slice (A) with a thin layer of silicone and adhere to center of plate. Use palette knife to remove oozed silicone from perimeter of agate.

4 Use traced circular outline as a guide to adhere assorted glass

nuggets (B) around (A) to fill remaining area of daisy "eye". NOTE *Center of daisy will not be a perfect circle.*

5 Form petals (C, D) using the opus vermiculatum method (p31). Following traced outline of a petal begin by gluing a perimeter row of tesserae within pattern line. Using a glass cutter or mosaic nippers, trim a tessera to fit into spaces not large enough for a whole piece (p23). When row around the petal perimeter has been adhered, start a new row within the one just completed. Use this method to fill in remainder of petal. Render each petal in the same manner.

6 Fill in remaining open areas between petal tips with random-size translucent green and blue tesserae (E). Set plate aside for 24 hours to cure.

7 Wash away marker lines on back of plate and examine mosaic from underside. If silicone adhesive looks unsightly, apply etching

cream to plate, obscuring adhesive by frosting the glass.

8 Finish by Applying the Grout (pp30–31) and Cleaning the Finished Piece (p31).

NOTE *This project is for decorative purposes only and is not suitable for containing food or liquid.*

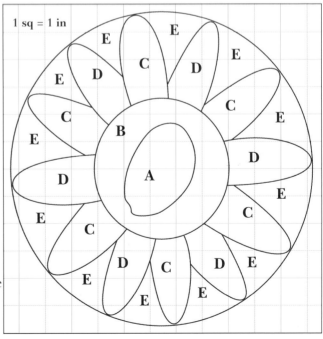

1 sq = 1 in

MOSAIC PANEL DIMENSIONS
10 in high x 13 in wide oval

MOSAIC MATERIAL REQUIRED

A 12 in x 12 in translucent light blue art glass

B 8 in x 8 in clear with white streaky art glass

C 8 in x 8 in textured translucent brown & amber art glass

D 10 in x 10 in clear, gold-pink, white fractures & clear streamers art glass

E 3 translucent amber glass nuggets (medium)

F 6 in x 6 in translucent dark green & white wispy art glass

G 2 in x 2 in translucent medium green & white wispy art glass

H 2 iridescent clear glass nuggets (small)

J 6 translucent red glass nuggets (small)

K 8 in x 6 in translucent dark gray art glass

L 8 in x 6 in translucent deep violet & pale purple art glass

M 6 in x 6 in translucent deep violet art glass

NOTE *The letter I is not used in this listing*

Letters refer to type and quantity of mosaic material used for pattern on page 106. The quantities and types listed are the minimum requirements for completing this project as illustrated, but materials may be substituted and quantities modified as necessary.

Butterfly Swoop
Window Hanging

Specific and/or Additional Materials and Tools Required

MATERIALS
$12^3/_4$ in x $15^3/_4$ in oval
  wood frame
11 in x 14 in sheet of clear
  4mm swirl patterned
  architectural glass
Charcoal non-sanded grout
2 small picture hangers
  and screws
Nylon-coated stainless steel
  fishing wire (20 lb test)
2 connector sleeves
2 cup hooks

TOOLS
Screwdriver
Needlenose pliers
Wire cutters

Base/Support Structure
A pre-made solid wood frame with a clear textured art glass insert is used as the base for this translucent mosaic window hanging. Any type of sturdy picture frame can be utilized as a base for a translucent mosaic by adjusting the pattern and material specifications. Refer to Preparing the Base/Support Structure (p95) for general information before starting this project. Specific instructions for the Butterfly Swoop are as follows:

1 The $12^3/_4$ in x $15^3/_4$ in oval wood frame has an opening size of $9^1/_2$ in x $12^1/_2$ in. On the back of the frame, a $^1/_4$ in rabbet (right-angled groove) has been cut around the opening perimeter to which the glass insert will be glued. Trim excess paper from the pattern outline and place the 10 in x 13 in paper oval face down in the frame. Verify that the pattern copy is the correct size and shape to fit into the recessed opening with the overlap resting on the rabbet edge of the frame. Adjust the pattern copy to fit, if necessary.
2 Place sheet of clear 4mm swirl patterned architectural glass (with textured side down) over pattern. Use a permanent waterproof marker to trace the oval outline of the pattern onto the glass sheet. Cut (p19) the oval from glass sheet and then place it into recessed opening of the frame to verify an accurate fit. Grind (pp25–26) or groze (p25) any glass edge that is too large for the opening. Once a satisfactory fit is achieved, smooth (pp24–26) any rough edges.
3 Set the wood frame face down on the work surface. Place the glass piece into the opening with the textured side facing up. Squeeze a slim

silicone bead into the corner of the recessed groove around the entire opening perimeter. Set the base/support structure aside for at least 24 hours while the silicone cures.

Mosaic Instructions
Construct the window panel by following instructions given for Translucent Mosaics – The Basic Steps (pp95–96). Refer to the photograph of finished mosaic to guide tesserae placement. Instructions specific to this project are as follows:
1 Cut and shape (pp16–26) all required tesserae as indicated on the pattern (p106).
2 Opus sectile (p31) is the tesserae style used. Individual pieces are cut, shaped, and laid out in a manner reminiscent of a stained glass window. Place the base/support structure over the pattern and begin adhering one glass piece at a time to the glass oval. Butter (p27) the entire underside of each piece with a thin layer of silicone and press firmly to the base. Use a palette knife to remove any silicone that may ooze out from between the glass surfaces. Once all the mosaic pieces have been glued to the glass oval, set the project aside for 24 hours until the silicone has cured.

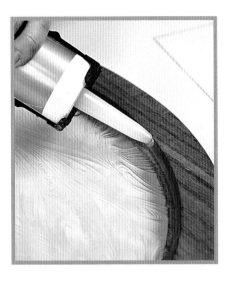

3 Follow the instructions for Applying Grout (pp30–31) and Cleaning the Finished Piece (p31).

4 Fasten the picture hangers (approx. 10 in apart) to the upper portion on the back side of the wood frame.

5 Use wire cutters to cut the required length of fishing wire. Thread a connector sleeve over each of the two wire ends and then loop each end through a hanger. Thread the wire ends back up through the connector sleeves and crimp the sleeves securely closed with the needlenose pliers.

6 Screw the cup hooks into the window frame, approximately **4** in apart. Hook the wire over the hooks to suspend the finished translucent mosaic in the window.

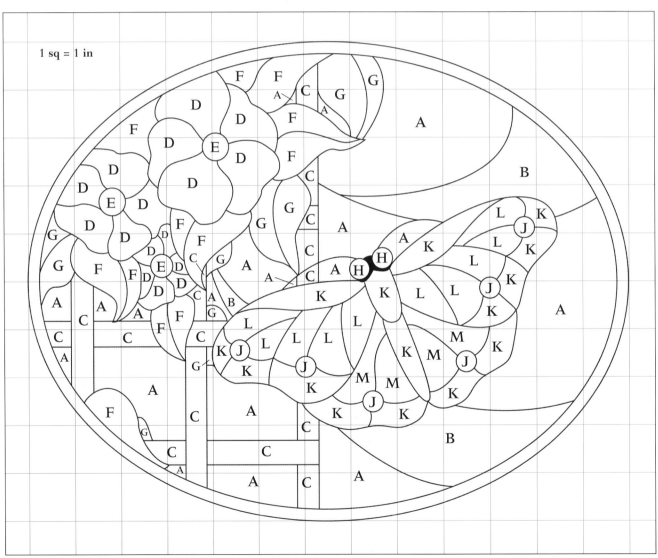

1 sq = 1 in

Dragonfly
Divider

MOSAIC PANEL DIMENSIONS
70 in high x 20 in wide

MOSAIC MATERIAL REQUIRED

A 20 in x 24 in clear 4mm architectural (Delta pattern) art glass
B 12 in x 10 in clear 4mm architectural (Croco pattern) art glass
C 8½ sq ft clear with green, blue, and purple fractures and green streamers art glass
   (cut into large random-size tesserae)
D 10 glass nuggets (assorted sizes and colors)

Letters refer to type and quantity of mosaic material used for pattern on page 109. The quantities and types listed are the minimum requirements for completing this project as illustrated, but materials may be substituted and quantities modified as necessary.

Specific and/or Additional Materials and Tools Required

MATERIALS
70 in x 20 in tempered clear
 6mm glass
Translucent purple art
 glass frit

TOOLS
Syringe (optional)

Base/Support Structure
Purchase 70 in x 20 in
tempered clear 6mm glass from
a local glass company. Order
the glass sheet cut to size with
edges seamed to remove sharp
edges. Due to the size, request
tempered glass (heat-treated).
Tempered glass will break into
small cubes rather than
dangerous shards if it breaks.
Refer to Preparing the
Base/Support Structure (p95)
for general information before
starting this project.

Mosaic Instructions
Follow instructions given for
Translucent Mosaics – The
Basic Steps (p95). See photo
p107 to guide tesserae
placement. Instructions specific
to this project are as follows:
1 Cut and shape (pp16–26)
glass pieces for dragonfly wings
(A) and bodies (B) and
random tesserae (D) for
background as indicated on
pattern (p109).
2 Place tempered glass sheet

over pattern and adhere
dragonfly glass pieces (A, B, D)
and then background tesserae.
Leave slightly wider interstices
($^1/_8$ in to $^1/_4$ in) between tesserae
to allow for addition of glass
frit. Butter (p27) entire
underside of each piece with a
thin layer of silicone and press
firmly to the base. Use a palette
knife to remove oozed silicone
between the glass surfaces.
Once glued, leave project for 24
hours until it has cured.
3 To maintain transparency,
divider is not grouted. Crushed
glass frit is used to fill
interstices. Use a caulking gun
or a syringe to squeeze a slim
bead of silicone between
interstices in one section.
Sprinkle glass frit over silicone-
filled interstices and press frit
into silicone using palette knife
or gloved finger. As each
section is finished, lift and tilt
base sheet. Gently tap
underside of glass to allow
excess frit to fall onto pattern
below. Put frit into a container

to use for the next section.
Continue in this manner until
all interstices are filled with
glass frit.
4 Allow silicone to cure for at
least 72 hours. Follow directions
for Cleaning the Finished Piece
(p31). A protective clear coat
can be sprayed over divider
surface to act as additional
fixative for glass frit. Follow
manufacturer's directions. If
the silicone appears unsightly
when viewing the divider from
opposite side, hire a glass
professional to lightly sandblast
glass sheet, obscuring adhesive
by frosting the glass.
5 Glass dividers can be installed
in a number of ways. If you
cannot install it yourself, hire a
professional. The divider can be
installed in a framed opening,
secured in place with wood
moldings or a metal channel
designed for glass installations.
For a touch of whimsy, pieces of
an old stair rail were welded
onto the metal frame of our
divider.

About Glass Frit

Glass frit is made by several art glass manufacturers and is generally used for glass fusing, casting, and blowing. Glass fusing (melting compatible pieces of glass together to form one solid object) has gained considerable popularity in the last few years so frit can be purchased at many stained glass studios. You can make your own glass frit by crushing and grinding pieces of glass into small fragments. This can be achieved by implementing one of the following methods:

• Wrap pieces of glass in heavy fabric and deliver a number of blows to the glass with a hammer until the glass is crushed to the desired size.

• Place several smaller pieces of glass into a heavy-duty metal mortar or bucket and grind glass into frit with a pestle or hammer head.

SAFETY REMINDERS Always wear safety glasses or goggles and a work apron. When working on large projects using silicone and other adhesives that give off vapors, work in a well-ventilated area and wear a respirator (if necessary). Always wear a respirator or dust mask when crushing glass into small fragments to avoid inhaling air-borne particles. For individuals sensitive to chemicals, wear rubber or latex gloves to avoid skin contact and safety goggles to protect eyes from vapors.

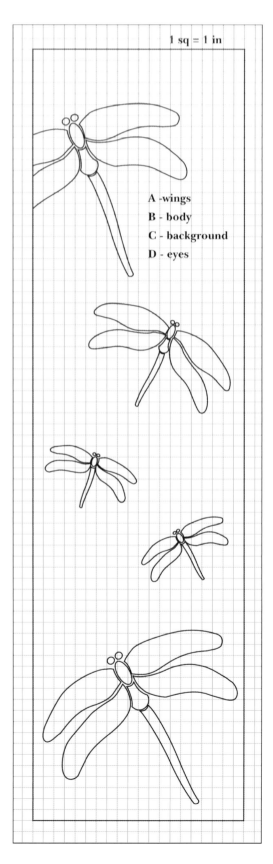

1 sq = 1 in

A - wings
B - body
C - background
D - eyes

Glass Mosaic Garden Stones

Beautify outdoor living spaces and flowerbeds with personally handcrafted mosaic garden stones. Give shady areas a boost of color; add interesting highlights to groupings of shrubs and trees; add shimmering elements to water features and ponds; or create a unique herbal garden. Whether one or a dozen, garden stones are fun to make and a joy to behold all year round.

The Basic Steps

The basic materials and tools that are required to construct the mosaic garden stone projects are listed below. Additional listings with specific requirements will be given for each garden stone project.

MATERIALS

- 3 copies of pattern
- Clear adhesive-backed vinyl
- Masking tape
- Mosaic pieces for project
- Newspaper
- Dish soap and water
- Petroleum jelly
- $3/4$ in exterior grade plywood
- Galvanized hardware cloth (wire mesh)
- Ready-mixed mortar cement
- Portland cement
- Water
- Liquid latex polymer additive (optional)
- Tint (optional)
- Sand

TOOLS

- Apron
- Safety glasses
- Utility knife or scissors
- Form/mold
- Permanent waterproof fine-tipped marker
- Cork-backed straightedge
- Glass cutter
- Tile and/or glass mosaic nippers
- Running pliers
- Breaking/grozing pliers
- Smoothing device – carborundum stone, wet/dry sandpaper, diamond pad, or glass grinder
- Small containers or jars
- Sponge
- Soft lint-free cloth
- Tweezers and/or dental tools
- Wire cutters or tin snips
- Rubber or latex gloves
- Respirator or dust mask
- Watertight mixing container
- Trowel or wooden straightedge
- Plastic sheet
- Spray bottle
- Razor blades and/or paint scraper
- Soft bristled brushes and/or toothbrush
- Small garden spade or shovel

The garden stone projects are made using Indirect (Reverse) Method (pp32–35) of mosaic construction. Tesserae are affixed to a sheet of clear adhesive-backed vinyl and positioned in the bottom of a form or mold. A fine cement mixture is poured into the form/mold. The cement mixture cures and hardens within a few days, becoming concrete and forming support structure that holds the many pieces of the mosaic in place.

Choosing a Form/Mold

There are many commercial molds available for making stained glass mosaic stones. Round, square, rectangular and hexagon shapes are popular and have led to the creation of many other shapes of molds - heart, butterfly, curved sectional molds to use as borders, etc. Household objects such as plastic food storage containers and baking pans can be used. Containers used for pouring a garden stone cannot be used again for preparation or storage of food. Patterns in this book may be adapted for use with most forms/molds. To make customized forms/molds, see the instructions provided for Making Garden Stone Forms (pp118–119).

NOTE *Any form/mold used for garden stones must have sides that are perpendicular (straight up and down) or at an outward angle to the bottom of the form. If the sides are angled inwards (towards the center), the garden stone and/or the form may be damaged.*

Choosing Tesserae Material

Correct tesserae materials are essential for the successful completion of a mosaic garden stone.

- The face (top surface) of tesserae should be smooth and flat. Use art glass, vitreous glass tesserae, and/or ceramic tile with an even top surface.
- When working with tesserae created from textured glass, tiles, or dinnerware, place the glass so smoothest side will form topside of stone. If textured side of tesserae is positioned to face the top, pieces may become partially or completely buried in the wet cement mixture. Air pockets between textures in the glass and vinyl create spaces for cement to ooze into and will lift the glass from the vinyl.
- Choose colorful, contrasting opaque materials for their reflective surface qualities. Keep translucent glass selections to a minimum, as they often appear dull and discolored when surrounded by the concrete of the stone. Iridescent glasses add shimmer and highlights, accenting features of a garden stone.

Preparing the Pattern

An accurate pattern is an essential step in making a garden stone. Follow these guidelines:

1 Make 3 copies (pp14–15) of the project pattern. Adjust pattern copies if alterations have been made to original.

Leave a space or line thickness of $^1/_8$ in to $^1/_4$ in between each tesserae piece.

2 Use one pattern copy as a guide for cutting, breaking, and shaping mosaic pieces to correct size and shape. Use second copy to cut out any pattern piece for a template (p16) that is required (e.g. when cutting opaque glass). Cut inside pattern lines. The third copy will be placed beneath clear adhesive-backed vinyl for a guide when laying out tesserae to form top surface of garden stone.

3 Verify the pattern fits within the form. Trim excess paper away from outline of third pattern copy. Place pattern upside down in the form so it lays flat and uncreased on the bottom. Garden stone patterns are designed to have $^1/_4$ in to $^1/_2$ in space between interior walls of form and tesserae along outer edge of pattern. If adjustments are made to the pattern for a better fit, adjust the other two copies as well.

4 Remove the pattern from the form. Place pattern face down on a light table and trace the design lines onto the reverse side. If a light table is not available, tape the pattern onto a window with design facing away from you. Use daylight to illuminate the lines and trace.

5 Tape pattern copy to a flat work surface or board, with reversed side facing upward.

6 Cut a piece of clear, adhesive-backed vinyl, $^1/_2$ in larger than pattern. Peel paper backing from vinyl. Position vinyl over pattern taped to work surface, with adhesive side facing upwards – do not stick it to the pattern! Pattern is completely covered by vinyl yet visible through it. Tape in place, do not position the tape within the pattern outline.

HELPFUL HINTS
Use clear 8 mil sandblast resist or mosaic mounting vinyl for strength of adhesive and thickness of vinyl. These materials are available at most stained glass shops and craft stores. Clear contact paper can be used as an alternative but the adhesive is not as strong and tesserae may not stick as well to its surface.

Preparing the Mosaic Pieces

1 Patterns featuring tesserae of the same shape and size will specify the number of pieces required. Cut the pieces (pp22–23) as listed for the project. Separate tesserae by size and color and store in small jars or containers until ready for use. Use the cork-backed straightedge to assist in scoring straight lines and tesserae pieces (p18).

2 Use a pattern copy and a marker to trace (pp15–16) distinctively shaped pattern pieces onto material to be cut.

3 Cut (pp16–22) each piece required, cutting inside the marker line.

4 Smooth and shape jagged edges or the piece may not fit pattern (pp24–26). Mosaic construction does not demand precision needed to make a stained glass window. Pieces should fit inside pattern lines, leaving at ¹/₈ in to ¹/₄ in space between each piece. Spacing allows cement mixture to get in and around individual pieces for a smooth finish and a good bond to garden stone.

5 Clean each piece thoroughly, removing traces of cutter oil, marker, grinding residue, etc. with soap and water, and rinse with clean water. This will aid adhesion of tesserae to the clear adhesive-backed vinyl.

6 Apply ceramic tile sealant to any unglazed or porous china tesserae surfaces to prevent staining and moisture retention. Allow the sealant to dry completely before adhering to the vinyl.

Placing Mosaic Pieces onto the Vinyl

The tesserae and mosaic pieces are now ready to be positioned onto the clear adhesive-backed vinyl. Remember, the pattern under the vinyl is the reverse of the copy used to cut the glass pieces.

1 Turn each glass piece over and place face down onto vinyl in the correct position. Press the pieces firmly onto resist.

Preparing the Form/Mold

Once all glass pieces have been pressed onto clear adhesive-backed vinyl, form/mold must be prepared before the mosaic pieces are placed inside.

1 Coat interior sides of form with a thin layer of petroleum jelly. All sides, edges, and corners must be lubricated to make releasing the garden stone easier.

2 Apply petroleum jelly along 1 in border around perimeter of bottom of the form, where sides meet the bottom. Do not coat entire bottom piece of the form or petroleum jelly will act as a large suction cup, making it difficult to release the stone.

Transferring the Mosaic Pieces to the Form/Mold

1 Use a utility knife to trim away excess vinyl from the outside perimeter of the pattern, trimming vinyl to fit within the mold without dislodging any tesserae.

2 Carefully lift the tesserae-laden vinyl and place in the center of the form with the mosaic pieces facing upwards. The vinyl acts as a barrier between the form and the mosaic and holds the tesserae in place while pouring the cement.

3 If form/mold is flexible, place a piece of plywood beneath it. Plywood/metal forms will not flex but plastic or resin molds will bend if moved or picked up before wet cement has set.

Trim away excess vinyl to fit mosaic within mold, without dislodging the glass pieces.

Carefully transfer the glass-laden vinyl and place it, face up in the center of the form/mold bottom.

Mix cement thoroughly then squeeze a handful. If it holds its shape it is the correct consistency.

Gently pat the cement to help it work its way into the spaces between the mosaic pieces and to release air bubbles.

Fill bottom half of the form with cement before adding the pre-cut reinforcement wire. Proceed to fill form, covering mesh.

Level off the cement using a trowel or a straight piece of wood.

Reinforcement

Before mixing and pouring cement into form/mold, reinforcement wire must be prepared. Galvanized hardware cloth (wire mesh) is recommended. Use wire cutters or tin snips to cut hardware cloth to fit within form/mold. Cut mesh 1 in smaller than perimeter of form to prevent wire from poking through the concrete on sides of garden stones.

Pouring the Cement

Use a fine grade of ready-mixed cement or mortar mix to acquire a smooth surface on garden stones and allow cement to work its way between individual mosaic pieces. Mixes with coarser grades leave a pitted surface. Pre-mixed bags containing Portland cement, sand, and various other materials are available at local hardware and gardening centers. Follow manufacturer's instructions.

1 Mix dry mortar mix to evenly distribute bonding agents. Entire bag (average size is 55 lb or 25 kg) should be well mixed to ensure a quality pour even if only a portion of the mix is required. Add and mix in 4 to 5 cups of Portland cement to ensure enough bonding agent is present.

2 Once the dry ingredients have been thoroughly mixed, empty contents of the bag (or amount required) into a water-tight container. Add amount of water required (about 4 liters for a full bag) and mix until the ingredients are well blended. Mixture should be moist but not runny or crumbly. The consistency is correct when a fistful of cement is squeezed and maintains its shape when you open your fist. Allow cement to slake (stand and absorb moisture) for 5 to 10 minutes, then re-mix thoroughly.

3 Carefully place a handful of cement mixture into the form/mold. Gently smooth

SAFETY REMINDER

Avoid contact of cement mixtures, whether dry or wet, with skin areas, eyes, and clothing. When mixed with water, cement mixes form a caustic, calcium hydroxide solution. Always wear safety glasses or goggles, work apron, rubber or latex gloves, and a respirator or dust mask when mixing and pouring cement. It is recommended mixing cement is to be done outdoors whenever possible. This will prevent the active ingredients and dust in the cement mixture from entering your work area and/or home. Any skin areas or clothing that come in contact with wet cement mixtures should be immediately washed with water.

cement around edges and over the glass, being careful not to dislodge any pieces from the vinyl. With your hand, gently pat mixture to release trapped air bubbles and to aid cement into spaces between glass pieces. Add enough cement to fill form halfway and continue patting for 5 minutes. Softly tapping a hammer or mallet on work surface also produces the same results.

4 Place pre-cut reinforcement wire onto cement and pour enough mixture on top to fill form. Again, gently pat for several minutes to release air bubbles. Entire depth of garden stone will be approx. $1^{1}/_{2}$ to 2 in, depending on form/mold used.

5 After patting for several minutes, a thin skim of water forms on the cement surface. This is normal. Level top of cement with a trowel or a straight piece of wood.

Curing

1 Set poured garden stone form/mold on a level surface covered with plastic sheeting or newspaper. Keep form out of direct sunlight and covered with plastic sheeting to prevent cement from drying too quickly. Leave undisturbed for a minimum of 3 days in temperatures not below freezing.

2 Once cement has set, mist with water once a day to prevent it drying too quickly.

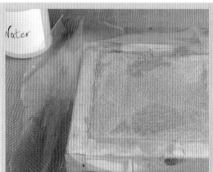

Cover the cement-filled form with a plastic sheet. Mist cement with water occasionally until cement is cured.

Unscrew the side pieces from the form base to remove the cured garden stone. Peel back the vinyl to reveal the stone surface.

Releasing the Garden Stone from the Form/Mold

1 Cover work surface with newspaper, turn over and lay face down.

2 How the stone is removed depends on the type of form used.

- For removal from wood forms unscrew bottom piece from attached side pieces. Unscrew two side pieces on opposing ends of the form so they can be pulled apart, splitting the form into two halves. Pull the two halves away from garden stone, releasing it completely from the form. To reuse the form, simply screw side and bottom pieces back together.
- For removal from molds that can not be taken apart, invert mold and lay it face down on work surface. With one hand, tap

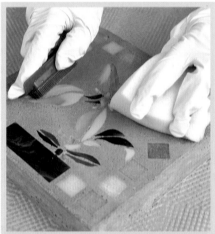

Remove the thin layer of cement from the garden stone surface with a damp sponge and a soft bristled brush.

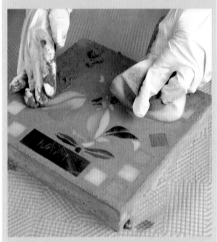

Small pits or gaps between the pieces can be filled by applying a small amount of mortar mix.

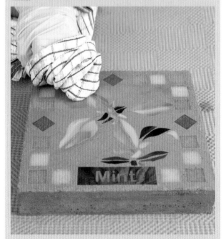

Buff the finished garden stone surface with a soft lint-free cloth.

the bottom of mold while slightly raising one side off the table with other hand. Rotate mold while continuing to tap until stone has released from mold. Do not use too much force.

3 Peel clear adhesive-backed vinyl from top of garden stone. With a water-dampened sponge or cloth, wipe away thin film of cement on glass surface.

4 Excess cement can be removed with a soft bristled brush or by carefully scraping it away with a razor blade, paint scraper, or utility knife. Use dental picks and toothbrushes to clear away bits of cement in the tesserae.

5 Small pits and gaps between tesserae are caused by trapped air bubbles and can be filled in. Mix a small batch of the ready-mix mortar and smooth over surface with a damp sponge or cloth. Add tint if it was used in the original pour. Allow mortar to dry to a thin haze for 10 minutes and then wipe away excess with damp sponge.

6 Remove continued unwanted cement from mosaic surface, with muriatic acid. Because of its hazardous properties, read label carefully, and follow all safety precautions. Muriatic acid can be found at your local hardware store and should be used only as a last resort.

7 Buff surface of garden stone with a dry, lint-free cloth.

8 It will take a minimum of 30 days for concrete to fully cure. Refrain from walking on garden stones or locating them outdoors if temperatures will drop below freezing until cured.

HELPFUL HINTS

Apply a quality water-repellent concrete sealer to the top surface and sides of the garden stone once the concrete has cured to help prevent damage and cracking caused by moisture and freezing temperatures.

Installing the Finished Mosaic Garden Stone

The garden stone can be set into the ground or nestled above ground amongst flowers and foliage. To set it in the ground:

1 Place stone in its chosen position. With a small garden spade or shovel, break ground around perimeter of stone. Remove stone and proceed to dig a hole $1/2$ in deeper than thickness of stone.

2 Fill bottom $1/2$ in of hole with sand to allow for drainage and tamp sand down, making sure it is level.

3 Place garden stone in hole at ground level to prevent visitors from tripping over the stone or damaging mosaic surface with the lawnmower blade.

Care and Maintenance of Your Garden Stone

Mosaic garden stones require little maintenance. Most garden stones can be left outdoors all year round regardless of the temperature. General care tips are:

1 Garden stones part of a water garden or exposed to a lot of moisture should be stored in a dry environment during periods of freezing and thawing.

2 Remove stains and mildew by scrubbing surface of garden stone with a diluted solution of chlorine bleach and water.

3 Water-repellent sealant applied to the garden stone surface may wear off over time. Reapply sealant on a yearly basis, according to the manufacturer's instructions.

Help! Why Didn't My Garden Stone Turn Out?

Before starting a garden stone, review instructions given. As with any home project, a less-than-perfect outcome can occur if all appropriate steps and techniques are not carried out. Here are a few tips and guidelines to follow, should you run into trouble:

Tesserae immersed in the cement

To prevent

Before being placed on clear adhesive-backed vinyl, tesserae must be clean and free of any cutter oil or residue from shaping or grinding. Avoid getting petroleum jelly (used to coat insides of mold) on tesserae or the vinyl when transferring the mosaic into form/mold.

• Firmly press smoothest side of tesserae onto sticky side of the vinyl. Wet cement mixture may seep between tesserae and vinyl if pieces are positioned with textured surfaces adhered to the vinyl.

• For strongest adhesion, use 8 mil clear sandblast resist or mosaic mounting material. Vinyl contact paper (shelf paper) with a strong tack can be used if others are not available. To maintain adhesive's integrity, refrain from placing anything but appropriate tesserae onto the vinyl.

• Care must be taken when filling form/mold with wet cement mixture and when patting cement to release trapped air bubbles. Patting cement with too much force may dislodge glass pieces from the vinyl.

To correct

• When tesserae are partially covered by cement, scrape away excess cement with a razor blade, paint scraper, or utility knife. Dental picks are useful for digging cement out of grooves in the tesserae.

• Tesserae completely immersed can often be uncovered. Check garden stone

When tesserae are immersed in cement scrape away excess, lift out tessera, and re-cement in place

Pitted surfaces can be filled by regrouting with mortar mix

Mosaic pieces can become dislodged if they are positioned too close to the garden stone edge or if cement is mixed improperly.

Always read and follow the cement manufacturer's directions carefully. Crumbling edges can be regrouted.

surface for a slight halo (outline) of the piece. Use a fresh razor blade to carefully scrape away cement until piece is revealed. Mix and apply a small amount of cement to the stone's surface to smooth out any gouges or unevenness caused while excavating a tessera.

• If the whereabouts of a piece is not known, it is advisable to leave it undisturbed. Once the stone has been situated in the garden or walkway, the concealed piece will probably not be missed.

Surface of garden stone is pitted

To prevent

• An interstice (space), at least $1/8$ in to $1/4$ in wide, must be present between each tessera to allow wet cement mixture to surround the perimeter of each piece and fill in spaces.

• Use a fine grade of ready-made mortar mix. If making your own cement mixture, use a fine grade of sand. Cement mixtures containing coarse sand particles may not be able to fit into interstices between the tesserae.

• After filling the form/mold with wet cement mixture, release trapped air bubbles and pockets by gently patting the cement or lightly tapping work table surface with a mallet or hammer for several minutes.

To correct

• Fill in pits and level surface of the garden stone by re-grouting. Prepare a small amount of wet cement mixture and spread over top and sides of the stone, forcing mixture into every crevasse. With a water-dampened sponge, remove excess cement mixture and smooth out garden stone surface. Allow cement to dry. A thin haze or film will be present on glass pieces and can be wiped off with a dry cloth as soon as cement has completely dried.

Tesserae have become dislodged from the garden stone surface

To prevent

• Cement ingredients must be thoroughly mixed and bonding agents evenly distributed throughout. Adding Portland cement to dry components will ensure enough bonding agent is present. Use a liquid latex polymer additive in place of some or all of water required. Store unused dry ingredients indoors, in a moisture-free environment.

• When transferring the sheet of clear adhesive-backed vinyl (with tesserae firmly attached) into form/mold, position the vinyl with at least $1/4$ in space between the edges of mold and mosaic pieces so they are completely surrounded by concrete and held in place. Pieces too close to outside edge may become detached or easily pried away from stone surface.

• Do not move a poured garden stone until cement has cured completely. Place flexible plastic molds on a sturdy plywood sheet for transporting to prevent tesserae from shifting inside mold and becoming encased in wet cement.

• Interstices between mosaic pieces should be at least $1/8$ in wide to allow wet cement to surround each tesserae and hold them in place. Very large mosaic pieces can lift or be pried off garden stone surface whereas smaller pieces are more easily held in place by the concrete.

To correct

• Tesserae that come away from garden stone surface can be reattached. Use a utility knife to smooth out inside edges and bottom of hole left by missing piece. Remove any debris in the crevasse. Spread a layer of water resistant tile adhesive on side edges and bottom of glass piece and press into the opening. Allow adhesive to dry for a minimum of 24 hours. Grout around tessera and opening with a small amount of wet cement mixture. Buff with a dry cloth once cement has set completely.

Edges of garden stone are crumbling and breaking away

To prevent

• Mix ingredients well to ensure proper adhesion and strength in concrete. Follow manufacturer's instructions carefully.

• Add additional Portland cement and/or substitute liquid latex polymer for water to supplement the bonding strength of the cement mixture.

• Do not remove garden stone from form/mold prematurely. Depending on humidity of local climate, concrete must cure and harden for at least 3 to 5 days. While curing, cover the form with a plastic sheet and mist with water once a day to prevent cement from drying too quickly. Keep out of direct sunlight.

To correct

• Try to strengthen the garden stone and improve its appearance by re-grouting. Mix a portion of the wet cement mixture and apply it to the damaged areas. Use your hands (wear protective gloves) or a trowel to smooth cement onto the stone and shape it to the correct dimensions. Cover with a plastic sheet and let dry slowly, misting occasionally. Once hardened, clean excess concrete off surface of any affected mosaic pieces.

Making Custom Garden Stone Forms/Molds

There are a variety of commercial forms and molds available. A number of household items can also be put to use – baking tins, spring-form cake pans, plastic food storage containers, etc. However, if a certain shape and size of form/mold is desired but not readily available, making one is easy to do.

Square & Rectangular Wood Forms

Wood forms are easy to make and are reusable. Wood is prefered for the construction of durable forms with straight sides (square, rectangular, hexagonal, octagonal, etc). All that is needed are a few woodworking tools and knowledge to use them safely. When using power tools, read directions and follow all safety guidelines. Always wear an apron and safety glasses.

MATERIALS
• 1 copy of pattern
• $^3/_4$ in exterior grade plywood
• 2 in x 2 in framing lumber
• #8 wood screws ($2^1/_2$ in long)
• Sandpaper

TOOLS
• Apron
• Safety glasses
• Marking pen or pencil
• Carpenter's square
• Straightedge
• Wood saw
• Power drill
• Screwdriver

NOTE *$^3/_4$ in exterior grade plywood is used for the base due to strength and durability. Plywood can withstand cement weight and not warp. A garden stone is $1^1/_2$ in to 2 in deep so 2 in x 2 in framing lumber is used for pieces that make up the sides of the form. (actual size of 2 in x 2 in framing lumber is closer to $1^1/_2$ in x $1^1/_2$ in). Sides provide support and contain wet cement mixture within the form until it sets and becomes concrete.*

Making the form

• Making base piece of form:
1 Measure width and height of garden stone pattern. Add 3 in to each measurement to allow room for attaching form side pieces, (e.g. 8 in x 8 in square garden stone requires a plywood base 11 in x 11 in).
2 With a marking pen and straightedge, mark dimensions required for base piece onto plywood sheet.
3 Cut base piece away from main sheet of plywood, using a wood saw.
• Making side pieces of form:
4 Measure each side of pattern outline. For each side piece, add $1^1/_2$ in to measurement, mark and cut the 2 in x 2 in framing lumber. For a square garden stone pattern measuring 8 in along each side, cut 4 lengths $9^1/_2$ in long.
• Aligning and attaching side pieces to base of form:

5 With pattern as a guide, lay a side piece along corresponding edge of garden stone outline. One end of the piece should start at a corner (where two sides meet at a right angle) with the other end extending past pattern outline, 1$\frac{1}{2}$ in.

6 Align next side piece. Butt one end of second piece against overlap of first side piece. As with preceding side, opposite end of the piece will extend past pattern outline by approx. 1$\frac{1}{2}$ in. Fasten the two pieces together with a wood screw.

7 Repeat step 6 to align and fasten each of remaining side pieces, creating a four-sided frame. Verify all four corners of frame are square, using a carpenter's square.

8 Place plywood base piece on top of frame constructed with the four side pieces. Fasten base to the frame, using two wood screws per side.

9 Sand rough surfaces or edges on the wood form.

NOTE *To make wood screws easier to twist in, mark and pre-drill holes in side pieces and base. Using wood screws instead of nails to construct a wood form allows user to take form apart if finished garden stone cannot be easily*

removed. Damage to garden stone is prevented and form can be screwed back together and reused.

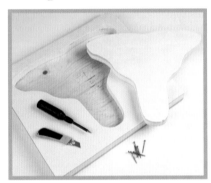

Styrofoam and Plywood Forms

Irregular shaped forms can be made with Styrofoam and plywood. High density foam insulation varieties, used by the construction industry, are preferable and are accessible at local hardware and gardening centers. Though not as durable as wood, plastic or metal forms and molds, these can be used several times when handled with care.

MATERIALS
- 1 copy of pattern
- Carbon paper
- Masking tape
- Styrofoam sheet (approx. 1$\frac{1}{2}$ in to 2 in thick)
- $\frac{3}{4}$ in exterior grade plywood
- 2 in drywall screws

TOOLS
- Apron
- Safety glasses
- Marking pen or pencil
- Utility knife
- Wood saw
- Power drill

1 Place carbon paper face down over center of Styrofoam sheet. Position copy of pattern with design traced on reverse side over carbon paper. Right side of pattern is facedown with reverse side facing up. Fasten in place with masking tape.

2 Trace outline of garden stone onto Styrofoam sheet. Styrofoam has to be large enough to allow at least 2 in of space between pattern outline and edge of sheet. Remove carbon and pattern copy.

3 For a clean cut edge, pull knife along traced outline in a steady and smooth motion. Do not saw up-and-down. Knife must be held perpendicular to the work surface and cut all the way through Styrofoam. If knife is angled towards center of sheet, undercuts will occur and will hamper release of garden stone from the form.

4 Remove cut Styrofoam from center of sheet. Verify project pattern fits within cutout.

5 Cut a plywood base piece the same size (or slightly larger) as the Styrofoam sheet.

6 Place the plywood base on top of the Styrofoam sheet.

7 Use drywall screws to attach plywood base to Styrofoam. Countersink screws so they are level with plywood surface.

NOTE *Apply a thin layer of petroleum jelly to sides and inside edges of all forms and molds, regardless of materials used in their construction. See Preparing the Form/Mold (p112).*

Garden Stone Projects and Patterns

Autumn Oak Leaf
Mosaic Garden Stone

FORM/MOLD SIZE   16 in x 9 in

WET CEMENT MIXTURE REQUIRED   12 cups per garden stone (approximate)

MOSAIC MATERIAL REQUIRED
A   16 in x 9 in light brown, dark brown, and emerald green streaky art glass
Letters refer to type and quantity of mosaic material used for pattern. The quantities and types listed are the minimum requirements for completing this project as illustrated, but materials may be substituted and quantities modified as necessary.

Specific and/or Additional Materials and Tools Required

MATERIALS
20 in x 13 in Styrofoam sheet
   (1½ in to 2 in thick)
20 in x 13 in piece of ¾ in
   exterior grade plywood

FORM/MOLD
Guidelines for constructing a mold/form like the oak leaf shape used for this project are given in Styrofoam and Plywood Forms (p119).

Mosaic Instructions
This garden stone is constructed following the instructions given for Glass Mosaic Garden Stones – The Basic Steps (pp110–115). Pieces are cut from only one type of art glass so consider how each piece is to be marked and cut, taking advantage of varying shades and unique grain (streaks and flow) in the larger sheet. The oak leaf stone in the photo is an example of the beauty that is found in a single sheet of art glass and how careful positioning of pattern pieces can enhance the overall design of a project.

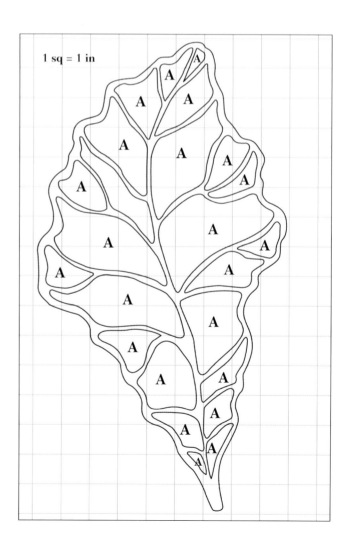

1 sq = 1 in

Luna Moth
Mosaic Garden Stone

FORM/MOLD SIZE   13$\frac{1}{8}$ in x 15$\frac{3}{4}$ in

WET CEMENT MIXTURE REQUIRED   12 cups per garden stone (approximate)

MOSAIC MATERIAL REQUIRED
A   7 in x 7 in black art glass
B   2 in x 2 in yellow with white streaky art glass
C   4 in x 2 in white with light green streaky art glass
D   12 in x 12 in light green with white streaky art glass
Letters refer to type and quantity of mosaic material used for the pattern. The quantities and types listed are the minimum requirements for completing this project as illustrated, but materials may be substituted and quantities modified as necessary.

Specific and/or Additional Materials and Tools Required

MATERIALS
20 in x 17 in Styrofoam sheet
   (1$\frac{1}{2}$ in to 2 in thick)
20 in x 17 in piece of $\frac{3}{4}$ in
   exterior grade plywood

FORM/MOLD
Guidelines for constructing a mold/form like the luna moth shape are given in Styrofoam and Plywood Forms (p119).

Mosaic Instructions
For this stone construction follow instructions given for Glass Mosaic Garden Stones – The Basic Steps (pp110–115). Moth wings are cut from one type of art glass (D) so consider how each piece is to be marked

and cut, taking advantage of streaks and flow of varying

shades of green mixed with white.

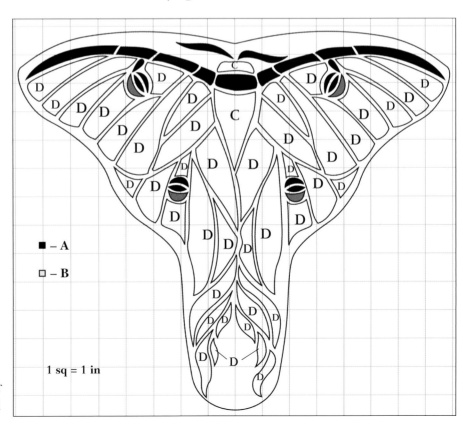

■ – A

□ – B

1 sq = 1 in

Basil Chives Lavender Mint

Lavender Chives Violet

Sweet Woodruff Parsley

Basil Sage Mint

Parsley Sage Sweet Woodruff Violet

Herb Garden Collection
Mosaic Garden Stones

Devise a unique setting that accents and identifies plants growing in your herb garden. Eight mosaic garden stone patterns depicting popular plants grown for their flavor, scent, and/or medicinal qualities are provided – make just one stone, a few, or entire series and arrange them to create a colorful backdrop for these beneficial plants.

MOLD SIZE
8 in x 8 in square

WET CEMENT MIXTURE REQUIRED
6 cups per garden stone

Specific and/or Additional Materials and Tools Required

MATERIALS
Heavy-duty masking tape
Glass etching cream (optional)

Form/Mold
Use an 8 in x 8 in square form/mold. Guidelines for constructing wood garden stone form are given on p118. When making more than one mosaic garden stone, make a number of forms so concrete can be mixed and poured at one time.

Mosaic Instructions
For garden stones follow the instructions given for Glass Mosaic Garden Stones – The Basic Steps (pp110–115). Also refer to photos of finished garden stones when positioning glass pieces. Instructions specific to this project are as follows:

1 Each pattern features a border of $^3/_4$ in x $^3/_4$ in square vitreous glass mosaic tiles. Lay vitreous glass tiles with smooth side face down onto clear adhesive-backed vinyl in correct position. Tiles can be substituted by making $^3/_4$ in x $^3/_4$ in tesserae from sheets of art glass. Refer to Cutting Uniform Tesserae (p22) for specific instructions.

2 Each pattern has 1 in x 3$^1/_4$ in piece of iridescent art glass in the center bottom border row. Surface of the rectangular glass piece is etched with the name of specific plant featured. Refer to the photos on p124 and follow these steps:

• Cover iridescent surface of glass piece with heavy-duty masking tape.

• Trace plant name on masking tape (see pattern p127).

• Use utility knife (with a fresh blade) to cut masking tape along traced letters. Do not press too hard and score the glass. Remove cut masking tape letters, revealing glass surface. The exposed surface can be lightly sandblasted to remove the thin iridescent coating to reveal the plant name. If you do not have sandblasting equipment, use glass etching cream purchased from craft and/or hardware stores. Follow the manufacturer's instructions to apply etching cream. Carefully wash cream away and remove masking tape, unveiling the name below.

Letters refer to type and quantity of mosaic material used for pattern. Quantities and types listed are minimum requirements for completing projects as illustrated, but materials may be substituted and quantities modified as necessary.

BASIL
Mosaic material required
A 5 grape purple mosaic tiles
B 3 sunshine yellow mosaic tiles
C 14 heather purple mosaic tiles
D 4 in x 4 in opaque light green art glass
E 5 in x 6 in opaque medium green art glass
F 1 in x 3$^1/_4$ in iridescent dark green and white wispy art glass

Specific Instructions

Form tiny flowers (A) blooming on stalk of basil from a grape purple vitreous glass mosaic tile. Use glass cutter or mosaic nippers to cut required shapes.

CHIVES

Mosaic material required

A 7 grape purple mosaic tiles

B 6 celery green mosaic tiles

C 12 rose pink mosaic tiles

D 4 in x 6 in medium green and white wispy art glass

E 2 in x 2 in medium brown and white wispy art glass

F 1 in x 3¹/₄ in iridescent dark purple and white wispy art glass

Specific Instructions

Form many tiny flowers (C) within two rounded chive blossoms from rose pink vitreous glass mosaic tiles. Use glass cutter or mosaic nippers to cut 4 tiles into smaller pieces and arrange them to fit blossom shapes on pattern.

LAVENDER

Mosaic material required:

A 4 heather purple mosaic tiles

B 8 celery green mosaic tiles

C 6 leaf green mosaic tiles

D 3 grape purple mosaic tiles

E 1 in x 2 in rosy purple art glass

F 1 in x 2 in royal purple art glass

G 4 in x 6 in grayish green art glass

H 1 in x 3¹/₄ in iridescent medium green art glass

MINT

Mosaic material required

A 10 spring green mosaic tiles

B 8 celery green mosaic tiles

C 3 leaf green mosaic tiles

D 4 in x 6 in medium green art glass

E 2 in x 4 in dark green art glass

F 1 in x 1 in medium purple art glass

G 1 in x 3¹/₄ in iridescent dark green art glass

PARSLEY

Mosaic material required

A 4 leaf green mosaic tiles

B 8 sunshine yellow mosaic tiles

C 6 spring green mosaic tiles

D 3 pumpkin orange mosaic tiles

E 6 in x 6 in leaf green ring mottle art glass

F 1 in x 3¹/₄ in iridescent dark green art glass

Specific Instructions

Parsley leaves have many small curves and scallops along edges. Nip away at edges with glass mosaic cutters, grind curves into glass pieces using a glass grinder fitted with a ¹/₄ in grinding bit, or cut the leaf shapes on a glass band saw.

SAGE

Mosaic material required

A 7 rose pink mosaic tiles

B 8 grape purple mosaic tiles

C 6 heather purple mosaic tiles

D 4 in x 6 in opaque green, purple, and white wispy art glass

E 3 in x 4 in opaque medium purple and white wispy art glass

F 1 in x 3¹/₄ in iridescent medium purple with white wispy art glass

SWEET WOODRUFF

Mosaic material required

A 7 sky blue mosaic tiles

B 10 snow white mosaic tiles

C 6 robin egg blue mosaic tiles

D 4 in x 6 in spring green art glass

E 6 in x 6 in leaf green art glass

F 1 in x 3¹/₄ in iridescent sky blue and white wispy art glass

Specific Instructions

Form the star-shaped flowers (B) from a snow white vitreous glass mosaic tile. Use a glass cutter or mosaic nippers to cut the required shapes.

VIOLET

Mosaic material required

A 7 leaf green mosaic tiles

B 9 sunshine yellow mosaic tiles

C 6 spring green mosaic tiles

D 2 in x 2 in royal purple art glass

E 2 in x 2 in medium purple art glass

F 1 in x 1 in pale green art glass

G 3 in x 4 in dark green art glass

H 5 in x 6 in medium green art glass

J 1 in x 3¹/₄ in iridescent dark green and white wispy art glass

NOTE *The letter I is not used in this listing.*

Specific Instructions

Form center (B) of violet from a sunshine yellow vitreous glass mosaic tile. Use glass cutter or mosaic nippers to cut required shape.

1 sq = 1 in

stems – D

Basil F

■ – E
■ – A

■ – D
■ – F

Lavender H

■ – E   rest of leaves & stems – G
■ – F

■ – E

Chives F

Mint G

Sage F

■ – D
■ – B   rest of leaves & stems – E

■ – G

Parsley F

Sweet Woodruff F

Violet J

INDEX

A Boy & His Dragon trio 75–82
– dragon bookcase 80–81
  – patterns 81–82
– shield mirror 76
  – pattern 77
– sword clothes rack 78–79
  – pattern 79
A Safe Place curio cabinet 72
  – patterns 74
andamento 31
adhesive 7, 28, 29, 33, 34
apron 13, 16, 23, 36, 109, 113
Autumn Oak Leaf garden
  stone 120–121
  – pattern 121
art/stained glass 5, 6, 14
Baby's ABCs wall plaques 39–40
background fill 28, 30
base/support structures 8, 28, 33,
  35, 95–96
basic techniques 14–26, 110–116
Basil garden stone 124–127
  – pattern 127
Birch Grove cabinet door
  panel 63–66
  – pattern 66
Blue-Eyed Daisy decorative
  plate 102–103
  – pattern 103
Bonsai tea tray 47–49
  – pattern 49
breaking glass on a score line
  9, 16–20, 22–24
breaking pliers 9, 17, 18
brushes 11, 31
buffing 29, 31, 37, 115
Butterfly Swoop window
  hanging 104–106
  – pattern 106
buttering 27–29
carbon paper 9, 14, 16, 28
carborundum stone 10, 24, 25
cement 7, 8, 13, 113–118
ceramic tiles 7, 23, 24, 30, 111
china marker 9, 23, 24
chinaware 7, 23, 24, 30
Chives garden stone 124–127
  - pattern 127
cleaning finished mosaics 31, 37
clear adhesive-backed
  vinyl 8, 26, 33, 111,
combination pliers 9, 17, 18, 25
concrete 13, 27, 110, 115
construction techniques
  (direct method) 26–31
  (garden stones) 110–116
  (indirect method) 26, 32–35
  (translucent mosaics) 95–96
contact paper 8, 111
containers 10, 11, 111
curing 29, 31, 114, 115
cutting glass 9, 16–22
cutting random-size tesserae 23
cutting uniform tesserae 22–23
dental picks/tools 11, 30, 33
diamond band saw 10, 20, 22
diamond pads 10, 24, 25, 68
direct method construction
  techniques 26–31
Dragonfly divider 107–109
  – pattern 109
drawing equipment 9
Dream wall hanging 53–56
  – pattern 56
dust mask 13, 109, 113

exterior grade
  plywood 8, 30, 36, 118, 119
float glass 16, 17
form/mold 8, 10, 110, 112–115,
  118–119
found objects 7
galvanized hardware
  cloth 8, 113, 114
garden stone construction
  techniques 110–115
garden stone forms 10, 110, 118–119
garden stone installation 115
garden stone maintenance 115, 116
garden stone preparation 14–15, 116
garden stone problems 116–118
glass breaking 9, 10, 16–20
glass cutters 9, 16–20, 24
glass cutting 9, 10, 16–20, 22–24
glass cutting practice patterns 21
glass frit 100, 107, 109
glass grinder 10, 24, 25, 26
glass mirror 6
glass mosaic
  cutters/nippers 9, 20, 22, 23
glass mosaic tiles 6, 39, 40, 115
glass jewels/marbles/nuggets 7
gloves 13, 109, 113
grout 27–30
grout sealant 8, 30
grozing 9, 25
grozing pliers 9, 25
hanging wall mosaics 37
Heartbeat wall mirror 67–69
  – pattern 69
Herb Garden Collection garden
  stones 124–127
  – patterns 127
indirect (reverse)
  method 26, 32–35, 110
interstices 8, 26, 27, 28, 31
Inukshuk Panorama wall
  hanging 70–71
  – pattern 71
iridescent glass 14, 111, 125
isopropyl alcohol 96
jars 10, 111
key(ing) 27–29, 33
latex polymer
  additive 7, 8, 28, 114, 118
Lavender garden stone 124–127
  – pattern 127
light box/table 15, 33, 111
Luna Moth garden stone 122–123
  – pattern 123
making your own cement 114
Man in the Moon Wall
  hanging 44–46
  – pattern 46
materials 6, 27, 32, 36, 95, 110, 118,
  119
Mint garden stone 124–127
  – pattern 127
mirrored glass 69
mitering 36
molds/forms 8, 10, 110, 112–115,
  118–119
mortar cement 8, 113
mosaic mounting vinyl 8, 33, 111
mosaic techniques 6, 26–35
mounting wall hangings, plaques
  & mirrors 37
muriatic acid 115
newspaper 12, 16, 114
nippers 9, 20
notched trowel 11, 33, 34
opaque glass 14, 16
opus 31

opus musivum method 31, 54, 59
opus regulatum method 31
opus sectile method 31, 61, 71, 88,
  91, 100, 105
opus tesselatum method 31
opus vermiculatum method 31, 45,
  68, 103
paint scraper 12, 29, 30, 33, 125
palette knife 11, 28, 29
Parsley garden stone 124–127
  – pattern 127
pattern copying 9, 14–15, 22
pattern preparation 14–15, 26, 111
pattern transfer onto glass 15, 33
pattern transfer onto base/support
  structure 28, 29
permanent waterproof fine-
  tipped marker 9, 15, 16, 20
petroleum jelly 8, 112
Phoenix garden marker 92–94
  – patterns 94
Portland cement 78, 113, 114, 118
power tools 36, 118, 119
Prairie Vista Triptych wall
  hangings 60–62
  – patterns 62
pre-or-ready-mixed
  mortar cement 8, 113
random method 31
razor blades 12, 29, 33, 35, 115
reinforcement mesh/wire 8, 113, 114
removing garden stone
  from mold 114, 118
repairing pitted stone 115, 116, 117
respirator 13, 109, 113
Rocky Raccoon wall hanging 50–52
  – pattern 52
Rose Nouveau tabletop 83–85
  – pattern 85
"running" 9, 10, 17, 20
running pliers 9, 17–20, 22, 23
safety clothing 13
safety glasses 13, 16, 22, 23, 36, 109,
  113
safety practices 13, 22, 109, 113
Sage garden stone 124–127
  – pattern 127
sand 7, 8, 113, 114, 115
sandblast resist 8, 33, 111
scoring glass 9, 16–20, 22–23
sea shells 7
sealant 8, 30, 115, 116
sectioning mosaic panel 33, 34
Serenity birdbath 57–59
  – pattern 59
Shining Stars wall clock &
  plaques 41–43
  – pattern 43

silicone adhesive 7, 95, 96
silicone sealant 30
slake 27, 30, 113
smoothing sharp edges 10, 19, 20,
  24, 25
sponge 11, 29–31, 115
springform baking pan 10, 118
stained /art glass 5, 24, 111
stained glass tesserae 22–23
stones 7
straightedge 9, 18, 22, 36, 111
Styrofoam garden stone
  forms/molds 119
Sweet Woodruff garden
  stone 124–127
  – pattern 127
tabletops 30, 83
tapping 17, 18, 20
templates 9, 16
terra-cotta 8, 30
tessera(e) 5, 6, 20, 22, 23, 26, 27, 31
Things with Wings
  bugmobile 98–101
  – pattern 101
thin-set mortar mix 7, 28, 30, 37
tile cutters/nippers 10, 23, 24
tile sealants 8, 30
tints 8, 114
tools 9, 27, 32, 36
tracing 14
transferring glass pieces to garden
  stone mold 112, 117
translucent glass 14, 15, 95, 111
translucent mosaic construction
  techniques 95–96
turning mosaic sections 34, 35
tweezers 11, 30, 33
trowel 11, 33, 34
utility knife 12, 30, 33, 115
Violet garden stone 124–127
  – pattern 127
vitreous glass mosaic tiles 6, 39, 40,
  115
wall hangings 37
wet/dry sandpaper 10, 24, 25
wet saw 10, 24
window tracing method 33, 111
wire/side cutters 11
wood base/support structures 8, 36, 37
wood garden stone forms 118–119
wood trim molding 8, 36, 37
woodworking tools 12, 36, 118, 119
work area 12
Wright Style duo 86–91
  – headboard 87–89
  – pattern 89
  – nightstand 90–91
  – pattern 91

Metric Conversion Chart

MM=Millemeters CM=Centimeters

Inches	MM	CM	Inches	CM
1/8	3	0.3	4	10.2
1/4	6	0.6	4½	11.4
3/8	10	1.0	5	12.7
1/2	13	1.3	6	15.2
5/8	16	1.6	7	17.8
3/4	19	1.9	8	20.3
7/8	22	2.2	9	22.9
1	25	2.5	10	25.4
1¼	32	3.2	11	27.9
1½	38	3.8	12	30.5
1¾	44	4.4	13	33.0
2	51	5.1	14	35.6
2½	64	6.4	15	38.1
3	76	7.6	16	40.6
3½	89	8.9		